P9-DGS-410

Lionel Trilling

Twayne's United States Authors Series

Warren French, Editor

University College of Swansea, Wales

TUSAS 523

LIONEL TRILLING
(1905–1975)
Photograph courtesy of Jill Krementz, © 1986

Lionel Trilling

By Stephen L. Tanner

Brigham Young University

Twayne Publishers
A Division of G. K. Hall & Co. • Boston

Lionel Trilling

Stephen L. Tanner

Published by Twayne Publishers
A Division of G.K. Hall & Co.
70 Lincoln Street
Boston, Massachusetts 02111

Copyediting supervised by Lewis DeSimone
Book production by Kristina Hals
Book design by Barbara Anderson

Typeset in 11 pt. Garamond
by Williams Press, Inc., Albany, New York

Printed on permanent/durable acid-free paper
and bound in the United States of America

Library of Congress Cataloging in Publication Data

Tanner, Stephen L.
Lionel Trilling.

(Twayne's United States authors series ; TUSAS 523)
Bibliography: p. 141
Includes index.
1. Trilling, Lionel, 1905–1975—Criticism and
interpretation. I. Title. II. Series.
PS3539.R56Z93 1988 818′.5209 87–21245
ISBN 0–8057–7503–X

For Liz, Char, and Steve

Contents

About the Author

Stephen L. Tanner, born in Ogden, Utah, in 1938, received his B.A. and M.A. from the University of Utah and his Ph.D. from the University of Wisconsin. He has taught at the University of Idaho and, as a Senior Fulbright Lecturer, in Brazil and Portugal. Currently he is professor of English at Brigham Young University, where he teaches American literature and literary criticism. He is the author of *Ken Kesey* and *Paul Elmer More: Literary Criticism as the History of Ideas* and has published widely in such periodicals as *American Literature, Shakespeare Quarterly, Studies in Romanticism, English Language Notes, Southwest Review, Modern Age, Essays in Literature, Arizona Quarterly, South Dakota Review, Studies in American Humor,* and *Chronicles of Culture.*

Abbreviations

BC	Beyond Culture
EL	The Experience of Literature
EMF	E. M. Forster
GF	A Gathering of Fugitives
LC	Literary Criticism: An Introductory Reader
LD	The Last Decade
LI	The Liberal Imagination
MA	Matthew Arnold
MJ	The Middle of the Journey
OS	The Opposing Self
PEL	Prefaces to The Experience of Literature
PMA	The Portable Matthew Arnold
SA	Sincerity and Authenticity
SLS	Speaking of Literature and Society

Full bibliographic information for editions used appears in the Selected Bibliography.

Preface

Lionel Trilling believed that objectivity in literary study and instruction "begins with what might be called a programmatic prejudice in favor of the work or author being studied" (*LD,* 226–27), and this principle guided his critical practice. It seems only fair, therefore, that his work be given sympathetic treatment. This has been my approach. I would add, however, that such treatment, in the case of Trilling, does not mean that his errors and limitations remain unexposed. As he stated on several occasions, the critic who is more concerned with the quality of life than with his perceptions about literature—the cultural as distinct from the exclusively literary critic—will make systematic mistakes, but they will be in the open, as will be the lively principles by which he made them. We should judge a critic, he said, not by his freedom from error but by the nature of his errors. Trilling's biases and limitations are easily perceived. In general he acknowledged them, recognizing they were a necessary adjunct to whatever truth he was able to bring to light.

For the most part, I have confined my study to the material collected in the Uniform Edition of the works of Lionel Trilling. This leaves out of consideration a large number of essays and reviews. But in light of the unity of concern in Trilling's work, the repeated themes and attitudes and the characteristic perspective, consideration of the uncollected writing would be merely additive rather than conducive to new insights.

I have not attempted a systematic explication of individual essays, which would require an inordinate amount of space and involve considerable repetition. Instead, I have tried to delineate the main concerns, assumptions, and characteristic methods that inform Trilling's criticism and fiction. This emphasis on central concepts unfortunately slights the detailed and subtle variations and qualifications of particular essays, but I hope it has the compensating value of explicating and clarifying the nature of his distinctive achievement. It seems an appropriate method to apply to Trilling, since it is essentially his own.

It is impossible to write about Trilling without using the slippery and emotionally charged words *liberal* and *conservative.* I am uneasy with these terms, but find their use inevitable. Trilling, in my view, has been identified too exclusively and uncritically with liberalism, particularly with liberalism in a narrow political sense. This identification has amounted to a preconception that has created distortion and misunderstanding in some of the commentary on his work, especially his later work. Despite his emphasis on politics, he was, in terms of partisan or ideological or practical politics, distinctly apolitical. His concern was literature and culture, and in his literary and cultural views he was singularly conservative.

I wish to acknowledge gratefully research time and money provided by the College of Humanities of Brigham Young University. I am particularly grateful to Diana Trilling and Jacques Barzun for permission to examine and use selected material from the Trilling and Barzun archives, Rare Book and Manuscript Library, Columbia University.

Stephen L. Tanner

Brigham Young University

Chronology

1905	Lionel Trilling born in New York City on 4 July.
1921	Graduates from DeWitt Clinton High School, New York City.
1923–1931	Contributes stories and reviews to the *Menorah Journal.*
1925	Receives B.A. from Columbia University.
1926	Receives M.A. from Columbia University.
1926–1927	Instructor, University of Wisconsin.
1929–1930	Part-time editorial assistant, *Menorah Journal.*
1929	Marries Diana Rubin on 12 June.
1930–1932	Part-time instructor, Hunter College.
1932–1939	Instructor, Columbia University.
1938	Receives Ph.D. from Columbia University.
1939	*Matthew Arnold.*
1939–1945	Assistant professor, Columbia University.
1942–1963	Advisory editor, *Kenyon Review.*
1943	*E. M. Forster.*
1945–1948	Associate professor, Columbia University.
1947	*The Middle of the Journey;* Guggenheim Fellowship.
1948	James Lionel Trilling born on 22 July.
1948–1961	Member of advisory board, *Partisan Review.*
1948–1965	Professor, Columbia University.
1949	*The Portable Matthew Arnold.*
1950	*The Liberal Imagination.*
1951	Editor, with introduction, *The Selected Letters of John Keats;* elected to National Institute of Arts and Letters.
1951–1963	Editorial board (with Jacques Barzun and W. H. Auden), Reader's Subscription Book Club; contributes essays to the *Griffin* (after July 1959 the *Mid Century*), the Book Club publication.

1952 Fellow of American Academy of Arts and Sciences.

1955 *The Opposing Self; Freud and the Crisis of Our Culture;* Litt. D., Trinity College, Hartford, Connecticut.

1956 *A Gathering of Fugitives.*

1962 Litt. D., Harvard University.

1963 L.H.D., Northwestern University.

1964–1965 George Eastman Visiting Professor, Oxford University.

1965 *Beyond Culture.*

1965–1970 George Edward Woodberry Professor of Literature and Criticism, Columbia University.

1967 *The Experience of Literature.*

1968 Litt. D., Case Western Reserve University; Creative Arts Award, Brandeis University.

1969–1970 Charles Eliot Norton Visiting Professor of Poetry, Harvard University.

1970 *The Life and Works of Sigmund Freud* (an abridgment of the three-volume work by Ernest Jones, edited with Steven Marcus); *Literary Criticism: An Introductory Reader.*

1970–1974 University Professor, Columbia University.

1972 *Sincerity and Authenticity;* Thomas Jefferson Award in the Humanities, Washington D.C.; Jefferson lecture published as *Mind in the Modern World.*

1972–1973 Visiting Fellow, All Souls College, Oxford University.

1973 Coeditor, *The Oxford Anthology of English Literature;* Litt. D., University of Durham; Litt. D., University of Leicester.

1974 Retires as University Professor; continues part-time teaching at Columbia University; L.H.D., Brandeis University; L.H.D., Yale University.

1975 Guggenheim Fellowship. Trilling dies in New York City on 5 November.

Chapter One
A New York Life
Philosopher of Culture

Lionel Trilling's death on 5 November 1975 brought to an end a writing career that began with a short story titled "Impediments," written during his senior year at Columbia University and published in the *Menorah Journal* in 1925, and ended with an unfinished essay, "Why We Read Jane Austen," written when he was a Columbia professor emeritus and published posthumously in the *Times Literary Supplement* in 1976. Between these dates, he published a remarkable number of reviews and critical essays, along with lectures, introductions to classics and anthologies of literature and criticism, a small group of short stories and a novel, book-length studies of Matthew Arnold and E. M. Forster, and four collections of essays. Most of this writing is now conveniently available in a twelve-volume Uniform Edition edited by Diana Trilling, his widow.

The obituary in the *Times* of London bore this headline: "A Literary Critic of Major Stature." This is an apt summary of Trilling's reputation, which remains probably as strong as that attained by any critic since mid-century. Trilling was the preeminent New York literary figure in the postwar period when literary study was the queen of humanities. In New York at that time, an era characterized by Randall Jarrell in *Partisan Review* as an "age of criticism," literature was studied with passionate concern for its political, social, and cultural implications. This was the approach congenial to Trilling and the approach at which he excelled. During the fifties, outside of New York, the New Critics enjoyed high prestige. According to Irving Howe, "Only Lionel Trilling among the critics living in New York did not suffer a loss of standing in those years."[1] In fact, John Crowe Ransom, a prominent New Critic and editor of *Kenyon Review,* actively and successfully recruited Trilling beginning in 1939 to write for the magazine and serve on its advisory board. The fact that Trilling continued as advisory editor for *Kenyon Review* until 1963 and served in the same capacity for the quite different

Partisan Review from 1948 to 1961 indicates his flexibility of mind and the breadth of appeal his thought and writing enjoyed.

Trilling is particularly recognized for his important role in the postwar redefinition of liberalism, and he perhaps exerted his greatest influence in the fifties after the publication of *The Liberal Imagination* (1950), but he continues as one of the large figures in American literary-intellectual thought. A poll in 1970 among intellectuals in the United States placed him as one of the top ten most prestigious contemporary American intellectuals.[2] William Barrett, speaking within the context of New York intellectuals, describes him as "in my view, the most intelligent man of his generation—or at least the most intelligent I knew."[3] In the opinion of Steven Marcus, Trilling's writings "are now a permanent part of our cultural heritage."[4] Douglas Bush says his place will henceforth be "akin to that of the Victorian sages and prophets."[5] In reviewing Trilling's *Sincerity and Authenticity* for *Encounter* in 1973, John Holloway asserts that "in our literary-academic world Trilling has to be called a heroic figure: almost the only one."[6] In his review of the same book, Irving Howe expresses the essential evaluation of many Americans who have estimated Trilling's reputation when he ranks him as one of "the two or three most influential American critics during the past thirty years."[7] Philip French notes that in Britain his reputation is "high and secure" among a relatively small circle of readers, but that there he "was never the controversial, emblematic, or charismatic figure he became—and continues to be—in America."[8]

One of the distinctive things about Trilling's reputation is the way he has been admired by nonliterary intellectuals. William M. Chace lists the following as people who have employed or expanded upon Trilling's ideas or otherwise acknowledged his influence: Richard Hofstadter, C. Wright Mills, Daniel Bell, David Riesman, Seymour Martin Lipset, Daniel P. Moynihan, Richard Sennett, Irving Kristol, and Philip Rieff.[9] This list could no doubt be enlarged. For example, the anthropologist Clifford Geertz recently acknowledged his affinity for Trilling's method of exploring the moral imagination.[10]

The principal reason for the wide appeal of Trilling's writings is that he viewed the study of literature as a study of human life and consequently brought to his consideration of literary texts a concern with large moral, psychological, and cultural questions. His encounter with literature often included but did not restrict itself to the critical act narrowly conceived as the description or analysis of a work followed perhaps by a judgment of its aesthetic merits. His deepest interest lay in searching for the animating attitudes and values underlying the literary work and weighing their moral and cultural significance. He assumed that a literary text is saturated with meanings relevant beyond the printed page, that literature has an important and determinate relationship to the real world, to the society and culture that shapes it and is in turn shaped by it. He regarded the patterns of living portrayed in books as solicitations aimed at the reader and ascribed to literature a purposefulness more than aesthetic. He detected in the artistically fashioned experience conveyed in literature intentions that, heeded by the reader, can mold attitudes, determine values, and affect behavior. He assumed that the literary work by its very nature is an expression of moral and social intent, and that to participate in its discourse is unavoidably to participate in the larger discourse by which the interests, purposes, and values of a culture are determined. For those who admire him, Trilling's chief virtue as a literary critic is his constant awareness of the social and cultural circumstances from which literature originates and to which in turn it contributes. Steven Marcus calls him "our historian of the moral life of modernity, our philosopher of culture."[11]

Norman Podhoretz acknowledges that others surpassed Trilling at close interpretation, demoting inflated reputations, promoting neglected classics, and literary theorizing, "yet the political resonance of his writings made Trilling stand out with a salience no other American critic of his time managed to achieve." Podhoretz allows that political undercurrents found their way into the work of other critics but insists that "with some the politics were so indirect as to be nearly invisible, and with others they were so dominant as to violate the principle of the autonomy of art." In the case of Trilling's essays, "The political charge was strong enough to electrify the mind and yet so subtle and muted that it never overwhelmed their independent value as literary criticism."[12] This observation is sound as long as "politics" is not defined too narrowly. Trilling himself subsumed politics under his definition of morality, having in mind "politics as it presents choices to all elements of the individual, including his imagination and his sense of the quality of his own being, politics as an activity in which the individual stakes all the cherished elements of his being on the chance of securing their safety."[13] Perhaps part of what Podhoretz recognizes as political resonance derives from what R. P. Blackmur describes as Trilling's "public mind." According to Blackmur, Trilling cultivated a mind never entirely his own, a mind always deliberately attempting to reflect what he understood to be the mind of his society. This required fortitude, says Blackmur, because it entailed an obligation "to take a position, to react and to respond, between incommensurable forces." Thus Trilling was "an administrator of the affairs of the mind," an example of "the rational mind at work to control the irrational mind in the name of wholeness, virtue, and humanity."[14]

Many agree that Trilling's basic concerns, though richly modulated over a period of fifty years, remained essentially the same. Those concerns have been variously identified and described, but perhaps no one has summarized them more effectively than has Edward Joseph Shoben, Jr.:

> His deepest and recurrent concerns centered on the struggle between the individual, striving for self-realization, and the culture that simultaneously nurtures him and ruthlessly bends him to its impersonal and corporate will; the precarious balance in our experience of freedom and necessity, the tension between personal will and the recognition of the world's intransigence; the perils of Utopian dreams, of fanaticism, of the damage that can be done by decent people who have no doubts about their own ideas, their own ideals, or their own commitments; and the uses of the imagination in dealing with reality, especially social reality—the reality of politics and of our cultural experience.[15]

To these four principal concerns could be added his preoccupations with death, the artist's adversary relation to his culture, the meaning of human authenticity, and the uses of "mind." His general subject repeatedly is the complexities and vicissitudes of the personal self in perpetual but generative unease with circumstances created by culture and history. All of these concerns participate in the two major intellectual quarrels Trilling engaged in throughout his career: with liberalism and with modernism.

Whatever concern Trilling addressed, he did so with a characteristic habit of mind, an inveterate dialectical propensity to weigh equally the opposing sides of every issue. When accused of having no position but of always being between, he said, "Between is the only honest place to be."[16] He situated himself "between" because of a deep and enduring conviction of life's complexity. This conviction or perception seems to have been part of his temperament, for it manifests itself in his earliest apprenticeship writing and persists to the end of his life. His wife and a number of his acquaintances have noted that *complicated* was for him a favorite and frequent word. "It's very complicated," he would say of most problems and ideas. Other words often found in his writing are *flexibility, variety, difficulty, possibility,* and *modulation.* R. W. B. Lewis identifies them as "the burden of his song" and says he was "irresistibly drawn toward any writing in which tensions serve to expand the world."[17]

Trilling was less concerned with definitive answers than with the subtlety, comprehensiveness, and energies of mind and imagination employed in confronting the questions. He repeatedly made use of his adaptation of Keats's principle of negative capability, the capacity to sustain doubts and uncertainties and to forgo easy or doctrinaire resolutions. As Tom Samet, who has written extensively and perceptively on Trilling, points out, he harbored no dream of "final deliverance from untidy complications, and he was wary of those who could not take pleasure in intermediacy, irresolution, the tug and pull and play of ideas. He knew that difficult questions are rarely answered in any ultimately satisfying way; he thought it sufficient to hold the terms of debate in a state of mutually sustaining opposition."[18] This habit of mind, largely a personality trait, was reinforced by Matthew Arnold's substantial influence upon Trilling. Arnold confirmed for him that conflicting principles could exist in permanent and vital equilibrium, and that very often such ambivalence of opinion was a proper condition of the moral imagination. The modulated sensibility, keenly attentive to the variegated phenomena of human thought and experience, was for Trilling a paramount virtue, sought by few and attained by fewer. The heroes of culture, in his eyes, are those authors with the fullest awareness of contradiction and complexity.

This doubleness of mind, this propensity for irresolution, has been seen as both Trilling's greatest strength and his greatest weakness. It informs his perennial anxiety concerning the proper relationship of self and society. The self cannot be healthy and whole in isolation from society, yet a self too conditioned by society likewise risks loss of health and wholeness. At different times he is both an advocate and an opponent of the conditioning forces of culture. Read in its entirety, says William M. Chace, Trilling's criticism reveals an "intense drama of cultural suspicion at odds with cultural faith."[19]

Family and Childhood

Lionel Trilling was born in New York City on 4 July 1905, son of David W. and Fannie Cohen Trilling. Both parents were immigrants. The father came from Poland at the age of thirteen under a cloud of family disgrace. Intended by his parents to pursue an intellectual life, perhaps as a rabbi, he had failed to perform adequately during his bar mitzvah in his native city of Bialystok. He may have suffered a lapse of memory during his bar mitzvah oration. If, as Diana Trilling suggests, the family descended from a Bialystok rabbi renowned for his learning, the degree of their humiliation is better understood.[20]

The family name may have derived from Wassertruendingen, a German town about thirty-five miles southwest of Nuremberg, which was called "Wassertrilling" by its Jewish inhabitants. David Trilling himself used to say the name was a shortened version of "Trillingwasser," meaning triplet stream.[21]

In America, Lionel's father became a moderately successful custom-tailor, but a subsequent attempt to become a manufacturer—a wholesale furrier—ended in failure, owing probably to what Diana Trilling describes as a weak hold on reality. He misperceived his market and lacked a sound money sense. His conception of what constitutes success and respectability was slightly incongruous with actual circumstances, and he was liable to fantasies of success, for his son as well as for himself. His public bearing was courteous and refined, with a touch of affectation, but among his family he also manifested fits of temper and hypochondria.

Lionel's maternal grandparents were born in Eastern Europe but emigrated to England, where Fannie, his mother, was born and educated in London's East End. When her mother died, Fannie emigrated to New York with the remaining family. She was sixteen or seventeen at the time and, as the eldest child, was required to assume a large share of family responsibilities. Consequently, she was deprived of the opportunity her younger sisters had to attend Hunter College. She regretted this, for she was an intelligent and voracious reader until her eyes weakened in her late eighties. Retaining a curious and flexible mind into her late years, she modified her views and opinions in significant ways throughout her life. She was a complete Anglophile and literary to a high degree. Diana describes how she would make self-effacing but perceptive critical observations on such writers as Stendhal, Thackeray, Tolstoy, Mann, Lawrence, and James. When Lionel was no more than four or five, she was reading Dickens and Kipling to him and announcing her desire that he should have an Oxford Ph.D. While this particular desire remained unfulfilled, he did become Eastman Professor at Oxford in 1964, a few months before her death, and her confident expectations and encouragement undoubtedly contributed to his literary and intellectual achievements. She was a vigorous presence in his life.

The Trilling family lived in modest circumstances. They considered themselves respectable middle-class people and assumed that intelligence and ability were as effective as money in achieving upward mobility. Although the parents could not provide their children with expensive experiences, they encouraged the life of the mind with a confident faith in culture and a lively hope for achievement. They viewed education not only as a way of economic advancement but as an end in itself. Somehow they helped instill in Lionel what Diana, in her biographical essay, describes as "an undefined feeling of personal worth, some secret quality of being to which he could give no name but on which he could ultimately rely."

Lionel lived as a child in Far Rockaway, which he described as "a comfortable New York suburb where a Jewish group formed around the synagogue an active community large enough to be both interesting and protective; at the same time we Jewish children were perfectly at home in the pleasant public school." His childhood was free from prejudice or persecution and he considered his family "fairly well established." Although orthodox in the form of their religion, his parents had a strong desire to partake of the general life and wanted the same for him (*SLS,* 198–99). Their emphasis was on the cultural value of Judaism and its accommodation to the best in the larger world.

When the family later moved to 108th Street, Lionel received training for his bar mitzvah from Max Kadushin, a protégé of Mordecai Kaplan at the Jewish Theological Seminary, where the ceremony was eventually performed. Kadushin described the Trilling home as Conservative rather than Orthodox. The house was kosher, and Lionel's maternal grandfather, learned in traditional Judaism, exerted an influence. Lionel's father encouraged him to lay *tfilin* while in high school and study Hebrew for the sake of Jewish culture. But, as he later said, "I did not get religion." He thought the traditional practices of Judaism did not fit his environment. They were like the clapper of a small bell installed in a large bell, unable to reach the sides and strike a meaningful sound. Therefore, he said, "except sentimentally, my parents' gestures could not touch me at all." He confessed being "bored and unattracted by the whole business." By the time he was in college, he was "one of the clever young men," free spirits for whom religion was not a valid thing.[22] In "Wordsworth and the Rabbis" he explains that his knowledge of Jewish tradition derives mainly from a work called *Pirke Aboth,* a collection of sayings of the Fathers, which he read in English translation as a student when he was supposed to be reading prayers in Hebrew, a language he said he never mastered (*OS,* 109).

There is an enigmatic quality about Trilling. Where did this mind come from and how did it create itself? If more biographical information were available, these questions could perhaps be more fully answered.[23] But even a brief outline of his childhood and family experience suggests the origins of some of his characteristic personality traits and critical predispositions.

For example, it is reasonable to assume that his mother's love of England and its literature was the wellspring of his own Anglophilia. The nineteenth-century British novel was the locus of much of his thinking. Those novels probably sparked his enduring interest in the social dialectic of self versus society and certainly provided him with the most complex and compelling formulations of that dialectic. He greatly admired the moral authority and standards of excellence of the British tradition and was fascinated by English social manners. As Alfred Kazin rather mockingly remarks, Victorian England was his "intellectual motherland." "This extraordinarily accomplished son of an immigrant tailor was so passionate about England and the great world of the English nineteenth-century novel that his image of this literature turned England into a personal dream."[24]

Mark Shechner points out that the intense strain of Anglophilia in Trilling was latent in the very home life and schooling of Jews of his generation. Noting the many Jewish academics who flocked to "English" after the war, he explains that it was not difficult for a Jew who had been indoctrinated at home in the values of prudence, thrift, responsibility, and achievement to be attracted to a literature so animated by a concern for individual will and conduct as the British, and particularly the Victorian. "It was the appeal of one culture grounded upon ethical precept for another."[25] This situation was accentuated in Trilling's case by his mother's birth and rearing in England. And the influence of that nineteenth-century moral tradition persisted to the end of his life. In a letter to Allen Ginsberg in 1945 he said, "You will have to understand about me that I am very largely an old-fashioned humanist, and although the humanist tradition sometimes exasperates me to the point of violence, I pretty much stay with it."[26] Robert Langbaum mentions a talk by Trilling at the University of Virginia shortly before his death: "He spoke about the will and how he considered himself a nineteenth-century person because he still believed in the efficacy of the will at a time when few other intellectuals did."[27]

Trilling's admiration for the British manifested itself in a certain affectation of style and manner. Several of his students and acquaintances have remarked on his refined aura, more characteristic of a thoroughly accomplished British man of letters than of a son of New York Jewish immigrants. His friend Irving Howe says, "this extraordinarily suave, elegant, dapper man didn't look or behave quite as if he were descended from the Byalistok Trillings."[28] A former student says "he was more Anglican than an Anglican, more aristocratically even-tempered and civilized than the real gentry."[29] But the same people who use words like *affectation, poseur,* and *persona* also describe the manner as entirely sincere and integrally adopted. Mark Shechner, for example, says that "the simulated English manner that was so integral a part of his bearing and voice was not just a literary taste or professional affectation; it was an identity."[30] It may have been this British-flavored personality that helped him become, in Kazin's words, "the first Jew in recorded history to get tenure in a Columbia English Department as crowded with three-barreled Anglican names as the House of Bishops."[31]

Actually, the grace and urbanity for which Trilling was noted derived ultimately from a source deeper than any model of the British gentleman. It originated in that sense of self-worth fostered by his early family life. That quality of being provided a certain confidence and stability that determined his character. Jacques Barzun, a close friend for many years, speaks of his "perfect civility and calm, even serenity" and adds: "He led a very respectable and modest existence. Socially he was not domineering or egotistical or eccentric in any way."[32] William Phillips says that, "except for occasional displays of personal or political anger, Lionel Trilling's person was very much like his writing: orderly, graceful, flexible, modulated, appearing in constant control."[33] William Barrett identifies his gracefulness as a moral quality, noting that even in the back-biting environment of New York intellectuals Trilling was not subject to rumors or scandal or personal defamation. He led an ordered life and enjoyed a long and stable marriage. "He was, to use the old-fashioned term," says Barrett, "a virtuous man and, moreover, a virtuous man without any touch of the prig."[34] Trilling, just as anyone must do, constructed his character over a period of years, but in his case a certain sentiment of being nurtured in childhood was the distinctive shaping force. It was this anchoring sentiment no doubt that enabled him to tolerate irresolution and find that position between.

Education and the Question of Jewishness

Trilling used the word *pleasant* to describe the public schools he attended. Jacques Barzun points out that Trilling attended those New York City schools long before they became "nurseries of illiteracy and vandalism," when they still supplied "excellent instruction and thorough preparations for college."[35] Trilling graduated from Dewitt Clinton High School in 1921. He recalled that he gained popularity during his senior year by a "Bohemian attitude," a stylish disregard for "scholastic pieties" and student "squads." The difference in status between those who were school personalities and those who were not, he said, revealing his typical English point of reference, was probably more clearly defined than at Eton.[36]

When Trilling entered Columbia as a sixteen-year-old freshman, he began an association with that university that lasted until the end of his life. Only a few years of teaching at the University of Wisconsin, Oxford, and Harvard took him away from New York City for any length of time.

According to Barzun, Trilling did not distinguish himself as an undergraduate. He seemed "content to do well, with little exertion, in what he liked and to stumble through the rest." He nearly failed to obtain the necessary credits for graduation because he was inept in math, "but a far-seeing mathematician-dean rescued him by legerdemain at the last minute." Barzun remembers that Trilling, in those undergraduate years, indulged himself in "a borrowed bohemianism" and affected "a languid, sauntering elegance (of manner, not of dress)." The manner, says Barzun, masked a "great shyness" which "persisted for a lifetime after the manner was gone."[37]

Trilling himself recalls in a personal essay honoring Jacques Barzun that during his first two years at Columbia he made a series of halfhearted attempts to take part in college life. He went out for *Spectator,* the daily newspaper, and *Varsity,* a literary magazine. Neither held his interest for long. He applied for membership in Philoloxian, the literary society, but was rejected. He won a part as a censorious middle-aged secretary in the sophomore show and knew after the first performance he had had enough of "student activities." He aligned himself "with a group of young men who held themselves apart in skepticism and irony; they could not properly have been called Bohemians and the category of 'intellectuals' hadn't yet come to be freely used, but 'intelligentsia' was available and on the whole appropriate, for they had, it seemed to me, a strong tincture of the young men in Dostoievski and Chekov; they suited my taste until I graduated."[38] In this statement, Trilling plays down his involvement in extracurricular activities in order to heighten the contrast with Barzun's student accomplishments. Actually, he was on the staff of the *Morningside,* Columbia's literary magazine, during 1924 and 1925 and participated in Professor John Erskine's literary society, the Boar's Head.[39] The entry by his picture in the *Columbian* for 1925, his graduating year, indicates that he had gained enough of a reputation as a literary figure on campus that the editors could tease about it. They identify him as one of "that famous group of intellectuals that tried to monopolize 'Sweetness and Light' a few years ago," accuse him of hiding his genius under a basket for two years, and reveal that "this master mind used to play marbles—in the dirt!"[40]

Trilling received an excellent literary education at Columbia. A significant part of it was supplied by John Erskine's general honors course, which played an important part in the life of the college during his undergraduate time. Erskine's course, which stimulated the general-education movement in the humanities, reflected the Columbia approach to education, which was intended to produce not a scholar or learned man but a well-read, intelligent man. The great word when Trilling was at Columbia, he tells us, was *intelligence.* In tracing his own development, he focuses on an intellectual tradition that blossomed in the twenties. It included men such as Van Wyck Brooks, Lewis Mumford, and Randolph Bourne, who were interested in the development of an intellectual class concerned with society and the idea of culture, both of which were thought to be malleable. This movement was based in New York and a number of professors at Columbia were part of it. Erskine provided a kind of slogan with the title of one of his essays: "The Moral Obligation to Be Intelligent." In this environment, Trilling acquired a keen and lasting respect for intelligence and, moreover, was converted to the assumption "that intelligence was connected with literature, that it was advanced by literature" (*LD,* 229–31). The "Columbia *mystique* of education," so strikingly expressed in Erskine's course, "was directed to showing young men how they might escape from the limitations of their middle-class or their lower-middle-class upbringings by putting before them great models of thought, feeling, and imagination, and great issues which suggested the close interrelation of the private and personal life with the public life, with life in society" (*LD,* 234). Obviously, the kind of education Trilling received at Columbia strongly influenced his critical concerns and methods, or so he believed.

Diana Trilling notes that a distinctive aspect of her husband's education at Columbia was the exposure to modern writers never mentioned in her classes at Radcliffe during the same period. Trilling and his classmates read many important modern authors as their works appeared.[41] No specific course in contemporary literature was offered, but the taste and stimulation for such reading were there.

After graduating in 1925, Trilling completed the M.A. in 1926, writing a thesis on Theodore Edward Hook, a contemporary of Byron. The interest in manners characteristic of his mature criticism is already apparent in this study, which Trilling intended as an exposé of a trivial creative life resulting from false and fabricated manners.

During his college days, Trilling recalled in 1966, he read the *Nation,* the *New Republic,* and the *Freeman* and was addicted to Wells and Shaw, but he had no framework or categories for interpreting society. He was trying to discover "some social entity to which I could give the credence of my senses, as it were, and with which I could be in some relation." He wanted some "ground upon which to rear an imagination of society." It was his discovery of the Jewish situation, through his association with the *Menorah Journal,* that at last made society available to his imagination (*LD,* 14).

He was introduced to the *Menorah Journal* by Henry Rosenthal when they were seniors working together on the staff of the *Morningside.* Edited by Elliot Cohen and Henry Hurwitz, the *Menorah Journal* was the monthly magazine of the Menorah Society. Its broad purpose was to further a secular, humanist, and progressive Jewish consciousness in America. It aimed to lessen self-rejection among American Jews by renewing pride in ethnic identity and history while at the same time reducing the feeling that Jewishness means extreme or alienating idiosyncracies that separate people from the general culture. Trilling's long talks with Rosenthal and his association with Cohen were for him a kind of higher education in Jewishness. In her study of Trilling's association with the Menorah movement, Elinor Grumet says that his later public pronouncements about Jews and Judaism "were the heuristic observations of these friends adopted by Trilling as conclusions."[42]

Trilling's association with the *Menorah Journal* lasted six and a half years, from the spring of 1925 to the fall of 1931—a period during which he graduated from Columbia, earned a master's degree there, taught for a year at the University of Wisconsin, did four years of doctoral work at Columbia, and taught part-time in the evening, extension, and day divisions of Hunter College. He published in the *Menorah Journal* eighteen book reviews, a personal essay, an essay in literary history, two signed translations from French, and four short stories, at least two of which were conceived as chapters of novels.[43]

Although he eventually became disenchanted with the pursuit of ethnic consciousness, for a time Trilling was keenly committed to a Jewish cultural renaissance, and characteristic attitudes of the Menorah movement appear in his early reviews and letters. In December 1929, while working part-time as an editorial assistant for the *Menorah Journal,* he spoke to the Convention of the Intercollegiate Menorah Association, presenting himself as a young Jewish writer saved by the magazine from diversion to other fields and a consequent waste of talent. In the same year, at Cohen's request, when its finances were low, he wrote a personal endorsement of the magazine. But when Hurwitz asked Trilling twelve years later if he could make public use of that letter, Trilling refused, saying, "those paragraphs were written in a special context which, for me, doesn't exist any longer and so for me they can have truth only historically."[44]

Trilling's commitment to the *Menorah Journal* was strictly social and cultural. It had nothing to do with Jewish religion, Yiddish language or literature, Zionism, or the flavor of Eastern Europe. In a way, it was a political act, for the arguments concerning Jewish self-realization were inextricably bound up with a general analysis of society. This larger analysis was Trilling's real concern, as it was for other young *Menorah Journal* contributors, many of whom turned to Marxist radicalism during the thirties. Consequently, Trilling's participation in the Jewish cultural program of the *Menorah Journal* provided a framework for applying his imagination to society and discovering a cultural politics. Anyone familiar with Trilling's work will recognize the importance of this turning point, which opened the way for his characteristic explorations of manners and morals, self in society, the conditioning influences of class and circumstances, and the interaction of literature and society.

Most of his contributions to the magazine were reviews of Jewish fiction. His characteristic method was to compare the work in question with the best of non-Jewish fiction, his principal concern being what universally constitutes significant literature. Thus this apprentice work actually strengthened his knowledge and understanding of Western literature in general rather than of Jewish literature in particular. Grumet believes his contributions attest that he "used the composition and criticism of 'Jewish fiction' to exorcise his ethnic habits of mind, by making those reflexes the subject of literary contemplation."[45] His standards of judgment were those of English literature, and he had already picked up the first-person plural of British essayists, for which he was later criticized.

Some of the concerns that would eventually become his trademark show up clearly in the *Menorah Journal* articles. For example, a 1929 piece titled "A Too Simple Simplicity" criticizes an author for treating life too simply. Trilling insists that life must be shown "to be dangerous, a complicated, a bewildering thing, full of paradox: a terrible, a strong thing."[46] A review of the same year titled "Despair Apotheosized" reveals his perennial preoccupation with self versus society and expresses the notion that despair, although a real problem, becomes sentimentalized by constant repetition and obsessive treatment.[47] These are exactly the same concerns that informed his essays forty years later.

In a personal essay published in 1928, he describes an image that persisted in his mind: "a rabbi whirling his arms excitedly so that the loose sleeves of his gown made a black penumbra around him." He imagines the rabbi expounding the question, "What does it mean to be a Jew?" Repeating the question over and over again, the rabbi each time emphasizes a different word in the sentence.[48] This is an explicit indication that while writing for the *Menorah Journal* Trilling was pursuing his own identity. One of the ways he did this was a study of the literary images of Jews. He intended this as a sort of prolegomenon to Jewish fiction and projected a definitive critical essay on the subject. As part of this study, he taught a course on the Jew in fiction in the Menorah Summer School in 1930. While preparing that course, he lectured on the subject to at least the Menorah Societies of Hunter and Adelphi, both women's colleges at the time.[49] An essay titled "The Changing Myth of the Jew," a summary of his summer course, was accepted by the *Menorah Journal* in 1931 but for some reason was not published. Trilling later remembered it as "inferior and dullish," but *Commentary* found it worth publishing after his death in August 1978.

It appears that the more he studied the Jewish identity the more he recoiled from involving himself with it. Ultimately he refused to implicate himself in Jewish cultural agony. In this he conformed with a general pattern among his generation. Irving Howe explains that the New York intellectuals were the first Jewish writers originating in the immigrant milieu for whom Jewish memories, either nostalgic or bitter, did not condition their self-identity. As early as the twenties, the dominant values in Jewish immigrant life were "largely secular and universalist," and by the late thirties, for the intellectuals, "Jewishness as a sentiment and cultural source played only a modest part in their conscious experience." They were more interested in breaking with their Jewish past and willing a new life. "They meant to declare themselves citizens of the world and, if that succeeded, might then become writers of this country."[50] William Phillips makes a similar point when he explains that Trilling's relation to his Jewish origins "was set in an earlier period, when one thought less of one's ethnicity than of one's internationalism and concerns for humanity as a whole. We thought of literature and our literary profession not as Jews, but as heirs of the Western tradition."[51]

Trilling's break with Jewishness was even more complete and permanent than was the rule among second-generation Jewish intellectuals. He acknowledged with pleasure the effect that a Jewish rearing had had upon his temperament and mind, but he recognized that the impulses of his intellectual life came from sources anything but Jewish and that the chief objects of his thought and feeling were anything but Jewish. He found the pursuit of cultural Jewish nationalism an intellectual dead end and conscientiously distanced himself from it. His subsequent criticism ignored the claims of ethnic groups vying with the English canon that shaped his criteria of excellence. Mark Shechner, who has displayed a keen interest in Trilling's relation to Jewishness, says that when Trilling made the break, "Jewishness was eclipsed, old associations kept at bay, the instincts soft-peddled, the unconscious squelched, 'authenticity' taken to task, and a curriculum of reading taken on as a prosthetic identity."[52] It is difficult to think of Trilling as Jewish at all. Apart from his early writing for the *Menorah Journal,* he seldom addressed Jewish themes, and the suave composure of his personal manner contrasted markedly with the restlessly combative style of other New York Jewish intellectuals, who, as Howe notes, were uncomfortable with gentility. "It was a device for making us squirm, reminding us of our uncouthness. And we repaid with contempt, as well as a rather ungenerous suspicion toward those of our own, like Trilling, who had mastered the art of manners."[53]

Disassociating himself from Jewishness cost Trilling some unpleasantness. Love of friends brought him to the *Menorah Journal* and prolonged his association with it after he had rejected its cultural aims. He was personally devoted to Elliot Cohen, who was protective of his young writers and had a great gift as a teacher. He stimulated Trilling and paid more careful attention to his thought and writing than any of his teachers at Columbia had done. When Cohen founded *Commentary,* he asked Trilling to serve on the advisory board. He refused, explaining his reasons in a letter to Cohen. He had had his experience of the intellectual life lived in the context of what Cohen called the Jewish community and wanted no more association with a Jewish magazine. Whatever such association meant for others, for him it could only be "a posture and falsehood." The young men on the staff were angry about the letter. Clement Greenberg, the managing editor, quarreled with him over it at a party, accusing him of Jewish self-hatred. They invited each other to step outside but then permitted themselves to be pacified.[54] The magazine pointedly ignored *The Middle of the Journey* (1947) and *The Liberal Imagination* (1950), but by the midfifties the breach was healed and Trilling began publishing in *Commentary.* He dedicated *A Gathering of Fugitives* (1956) to Cohen and delivered his eulogy in 1959.

Jewishness for Trilling was never a matter of religious observance, traditional texts, Jewish history and languages, or Zionist feeling. It was a social fact. He said to the Jewish Student Society at Columbia in 1939, "The meaning of Jewishness lies largely with the action of non-Jews. It is not a racial fact; it is not a religious fact to any great extent, it is not a positive cultural fact. It is wholly a social fact."[55] He reiterated this point in 1944 when asked to participate in a symposium on American Literature and the Younger Generation of American Jews in the *Contemporary Jewish Record:* "As I see it, the great fact for American Jews is their exclusion from certain parts of the general life and every activity of Jewish life seems to be a response to this fact." He recoiled from the negative nature of this "fact," feeling that it prevented the Jewish religion from fostering positive achievements: "Modern Jewish religion at its best may indeed be intelligent and soaked in university knowledge, but out of it there has not come a single voice with the note of authority—of philosophical, or poetic, or even of rhetorical, let alone of religious, authority" (*SLS,* 200).

His disclaimer regarding Jewishness is firm and unequivocal. While admitting that it is never possible for a Jew of his generation to "escape" his Jewish origin, he insists that "I cannot discover anything in my professional intellectual life which I can specifically trace back to my Jewish birth and rearing. I do not think of myself as a 'Jewish writer.' I do not have it in mind to serve by my writing any Jewish purpose. I should resent it if a critic of my work were to discover in it either faults or virtues which he called Jewish" (*SLS,* 199). It is possible that Trilling's deeply imbued suspicion of the powerful conditioning force of culture upon the individual self was partly instilled in him by his youthful experience with programmatic Jewish consciousness.

Teacher and Critic

After receiving his M.A. in 1926, Trilling spent a year as an instructor in Alexander Meiklejohn's experimental college at the University of Wisconsin. He was too much a New Yorker to feel at home in a Midwestern college town. Kazin describes him once telling, with a wave of the arm as though indicating the great beyond, that he went way out there to Wisconsin to teach for a year. According to Kazin, Trilling considered it a sort of exile from Columbia.[56] Moreover, when he went to Madison, he was struggling with the question of his Jewish identity, and the non-Jewish environment there exacerbated that self-consciousness. It is not surprising that by early spring in 1927 he was impatient to return to New York. In expressing that impatience in a letter to Barzun, he said, "Madison is a funny town. I try to understand it and do, a little, but it still retains its droll incomprehensibility for me. It has a code and civilization of its own, fairly sophisticated and rather presentable, but subtly and rigidly its own. It would need a novel, of course, to explain it."[57] He never wrote such a novel, but several of his short stories and a personal essay grew out of that year in Madison.

Some have charged that Trilling never developed much comprehension of American life outside of New York City, that he never saw what he himself called "the American reality" steadily and whole. W. M. Frohock, for example, claims that Trilling's perspective from Morningside Heights was "curiously foreshortened." Some rather marked aspects of the hinterland, certain regional differences and cultural variations, escaped his vision. Consequently, argues Frohock, he spoke mainly to a group of intellectuals whose spiritual home was New York City regardless of where they lived.[58] The accuracy of this charge may be arguable, but when Trilling returned to New York he stayed there, with brief exceptions, for the rest of his life, and one searches his criticism in vain for any significant consideration of the "droll incomprehensibility" of heartland America.

The next years were strenuous for him. Diana Trilling describes them in "Lionel Trilling: A Jew at Columbia." Early in 1928 he began teaching evening and extension sessions at Hunter College, an unsatisfying part-time association that continued until 1934. He married Diana Rubin in June 1929 and worked part-time on the staff of the *Menorah Journal* during the following year. Apparently this work also was less than satisfying. His wife says he preferred not to discuss it, and he did not mention it in print until years later. Many of his associates in the New York intellectual community were unaware of his connection with the *Menorah Journal* until his mature years. A fellowship and the offer of an instructorship at Columbia in 1932 gave hope and direction to his career, but scarcely eased his financial distress. His father's fur business had failed and Trilling was burdened with supporting his family. Diana's father had been impoverished in the 1929 stock market crash, and she became seriously ill with hyperthyroidism, which meant an added expense for ten years. As an instructor, Trilling taught four full courses while working on his Ph.D., doing book reviews and literary odd jobs to earn much-needed money. His later self-possession and urbanity, suggesting social privilege in youth, would belie his insecurity and financial tribulations during those depression years.

The appointment to an instructorship was surprising and rather inexplicable given the restricted opportunities for Jews in higher education at the time. "When I decided to go into academic life," Trilling recalls in his essay on being young in the thirties, "my friends thought me naive to the point of absurdity, nor were they wholly wrong—my appointment to an instructorship in Columbia College was pretty openly regarded as an experiment, and for some time my career in the College was conditioned by my being Jewish" (*LD,* 13). Apparently Ashley Thorndike, then head of the department, wanted to test a Jew, and Trilling seemed a good risk in appearance and name. Diana speculates that "had his name been that of his maternal grandfather, Israel Cohen, it is highly questionable whether the offer would have been made" (*SLS,* 421). He taught for four years, working with only partial success on a dissertation on Matthew Arnold under the direction of Emory Neff, a specialist in Carlyle and Mill. At the end of that time he was let go, the department spokesman suggesting that "as a Freudian, a Marxist, and a Jew" he would be "more comfortable" elsewhere.[59]

In reality, Trilling in 1936 was none of these things in a marked degree. He had not yet written of Freud or read the particular books of Freud that would later have such extraordinary impact on his thought. As for his Marxism, in July 1935 he had written to Barzun that the publications of the Communist Party were descending to an ever lower level and he wanted no place in the active Left. "But when the book [the dissertation on Matthew Arnold] is finished I want to learn Marxism. Partly because I think we cannot teach our best students—mostly Marxist—until we know a great deal more than they do about their religious conversions. And I know very little."[60] In some autobiographical notes made late in life, he says, "Only for a very short time, and then quite presumptuously, did I think of myself as a Marxist" (*LD*, 237). And, as far as being a Jew is concerned, by 1936 his experiment with cultivating a conscious Jewish identity was, of course, irrevocably behind him.

He was devastated by the dismissal, but in a few days took the most decisive action of his life.[61] Its source, suggests Diana, was his mother's insistent expectations for him. He confronted each of the department members he knew best. "He didn't reason with them, he didn't argue with them. He told them that they were getting rid of a person who would one day bring great distinction to their department; they would not easily find another as good" (*SLS*, 424). This uncharacteristic transformation, this startling new show of confident self-possession, worked the miracle. He was reappointed for another year, which multiplied because he was a changed person. The problems with shaping his book on Arnold disappeared immediately. In 1939 it was published and he was promoted to assistant professor of English, the first Jew of that department to become a member of the faculty. Additional promotions and distinguished appointments followed in order: associate professor in 1945, professor in 1948, George Edward Woodberry Professor of Literature and Criticism in 1965, and University Professor in 1970, the highest distinction Columbia University confers on a member of its faculty.

In the fall of 1934, Trilling and Barzun began teaching together a colloquium on great books. This course, emphasizing the social and cultural relationships of literature and ideas, they continued for nearly forty years, and it became something of a legend for its high-spirited intellectual exchanges. It followed the pattern of John Erskine's general honors course—a small class with two instructors of different disciplines meeting for two hours one evening a week—which both Trilling and

Barzun held "in pious memory" from their undergraduate days. The two teachers differed widely in taste, but they shared a common view of life that enabled them to diverge in style and purpose while presenting a unified mode of "cultural criticism" to their students. Barzun explains that this common view of life originated in the recognition that "ideologies and coercive systems" not only leave much of life out of account but destroy the very things worth cherishing. "In other words, variety and complexity are but different names for possibility; and without possibility—freedom for the unplanned and indefinite—life becomes a savourless round of predictable acts."[62]

The friendship between these two renowned educators was enduring and mutually supportive to a rare degree. During their lifetime association, they graciously and conscientiously read each other's manuscripts with a warm respect for each other's opinions.

Trilling was a potent influence in the English Department at Columbia. Irving Howe characterizes him along with T. S. Eliot, Yvor Winters, F. R. Leavis, John Crowe Ransom, and Richard Blackmur as "not attendant lords waiting upon princes of the imagination," but as "powerful dukes and barons ruling their own demesnes. . . . And each year there poured out eager followers from the graduate schools, loyal to master and method."[63] Although teaching was always his primary commitment and great love, his influence perhaps derived more from his writing than from his teaching. He was more effective at his writing desk than at the lectern. The common report from his students is that he was not an effective lecturer. He lacked the scintillating delivery that other popular professors enjoyed and sometimes gave the impression of great intelligence unable to present itself to a student audience. "Weariness was the dominant message of his physical presence," remembers one former student, but he also had moments of "almost naughty enthusiasm" when he would digress. His lecture method was rather impressionistic. "He would approach the day's text gingerly, as if not to alarm its mystery by asking it to disrobe too quickly. He might circle around it first with biographical detail or plot telling, but he would always work back in the course of the hour to an effort to capture the heart of the book." Occasionally he turned from lecturing to try to generate discussion, but this seldom worked. The first stupid comment would put him off. "He was not like those professors who love to play Socrates, gleefully drawing out truth from student errors. Trilling, faced with the job of reforming human ignorance, would often as not retreat, or leave as is."[64]

The lack of a vivacious classroom manner was compensated for by other qualities. Kindness and courtesy marked his relationship with students. Philip Lopate says he was "disarmingly and off-handedly good. And very vulnerable, too, in his anxious desire that we be gentle with each other."[65] Norman Podhoretz, once his student, says Trilling, as a teacher, tended to be tolerant and relaxed about differences of opinion concerning literature, partly because he never felt literature was all-important in life; other things mattered as well.[66] But this tolerance and this moderate perspective on the importance of literature were not signs of a lukewarm commitment to literary study. Quite the contrary was true. He demonstrated to his students that the study of English is a serious matter. As John Hollander, also a former student, puts it, he was a reversal of the stereotype of the English professor: "instead of a rather clerical, scholarly sort of person here was somebody implicitly and consistently arguing by his concerns, and by the unique quality of his seriousness, that being a professor of literature might amount to one of the few remaining pursuits worth following."[67] Literature is not the only thing that matters, he taught, but it is the best way to get at things that do matter.

Another endearing quality of his teaching was his honesty and modesty about his own limits. One former student remembers him addressing a class of two hundred for an hour about how he had puzzled for several days over Kafka's *The Trial* without finding the inspiration for a coherent interpretation.[68] Lopate thinks one of his finest hours was when he had assigned, before reading it, Camus's *The Rebel* as the final, summing-up text for a course in modernism. After reading it, he confessed to his class that he "couldn't make head or tail of it." Everything was either too obvious or else impenetrable, so he struck it from the reading list.[69]

Trilling's career as a critic, begun with the *Menorah Journal,* shifted direction as he began to write for the *New Republic, New Freeman,* and *Nation* in 1930 and ceased writing for the *Menorah Journal* in 1931. For a while, like many of his contemporaries, he turned his thoughts to social and economic change and was curious about Marxism. He aligned himself with the left-wing intelligentsia during the early depression. In the introduction to *The Middle of the Journey,* he says, "we were a group who, for a short time in 1932 and even into 1933, had been in a tenuous relation with the Communist Party through some of its so-called fringe activities" (*MJ,* xvi). But he was disillusioned early with the Party and the cruder forms of Marxism. He complained to Barzun in 1937 about an article in the *New Republic,* the author of which "writes a kind of polite vulgar-Marxism which goes down with intellectual liberals so easy and which I conceive it my job in the future to destroy. I find no intellectual position more grateful to me than that of trying to keep the walls of the Right and the Left from coming together to squash me, like the ? Poe story."[70]

In the midthirties he held some sympathy with Trotskyism, but thought it without power. His interest in the Trotskyist position had more to do with its offering a critique of the Communist Party than with its offering an alternative party line. Its attraction lay in its nonpolitical character. It was simply a way of saying no to Stalin's Soviet Union. From the time of Trotsky's banishment in 1929, Trilling distrusted and feared Stalinism, and this antipathy never lessened. Throughout his career he resisted systems, either aesthetic or political. They were for him the sign of a mind not fully cultivated, and Stalinism in his eyes was always the most alarming example of their nature and consequences. His persistent antagonism toward Stalinism was not a political position per se, and he proposed no alternative political organization. His position was essentially a literary and cultural perspective for illuminating the dangers and inadequacies of Stalinism and what it represented.

His political "activities" in the thirties consisted mainly in writing letters to the editor and signing petitions. For example, in 1934 he and several others wrote a letter to the Communist Party protesting their effort to break up a Socialist rally at Madison Square Garden.[71] Increasingly in the thirties he manifested a detachment from political activism and an inclination to treat literature on the basis of its own cogency and adequacy in treating life's complexities rather than for its relevance to class struggle. If he desired the emergence of any class, it was not the proletariat, but rather an intellectual class capable of realizing humanistic ideals in society. His 1939 essay "Hemingway and His Critics" (*SLS,* 123–34) is a forceful rejection of the liberal-radical assumptions about the function of literature as an instrument of class struggle or political propaganda. His study of literature, particularly his intensive study of Matthew Arnold during the thirties, insulated him from his politically active contemporaries' tendency toward ideological shifts and upheavals. Consequently he was less involved and more discerning, more a critical observer than a participant.

Trilling admitted that the writings of Marx had a decisive influence on his intellectual life, but it was Marx's method more than his conclusions that interested him. Barzun points out that Trilling's Marxism was always a sort of "cultural creed." He went to the early Marx for something more wide open and generous than the formulations following the 1859 *Critique of Political Economy.* "As his awareness of the practical embodiments of Marxism grew sharper and more intense he fell away not from Marx's revelations, so to speak, but from the machinery, the structure and the system."[72] Actually, little Marxism is to be found in his writings, unless historicism and determinism and a strong interest in the manners and customs of class are to be considered Marxist. But these concerns predate Marx, and Trilling does not address them in a specifically Marxist framework.

As in the case of his experience with programmatic Jewishness, his radicalism was rootless and faded quickly from his life, contributing to his characteristic distrust of limiting programs and systems.

By the time his book on Arnold appeared in 1939, he had published nearly fifty articles in addition to the twenty-odd items in the *Menorah Journal.* Most of these appeared in the *Nation* and *New Republic,* a few in *Partisan Review.* In a letter to Barzun in June of that year, he confides that he has some difficulties to overcome: "Not the least of them is the understanding that my too long apprenticeship is over and that I now can and must speak out; and on the other hand, when moments of that understanding come, that I must not let it frighten me into silence."[73] He did speak out, and the forties were a productive time for him. He continued frequent publication in the *Nation, New Republic,* and *Partisan Review,* and began a long association with *Kenyon Review.* In 1943 he published *E. M. Forster* and his famous story "Of This Time, Of That Place." Another story, "The Other Margaret," appeared in 1945 and *The Middle of the Journey* in 1947. "The Lesson and the Secret" appeared in 1949 along with *The Portable Matthew Arnold.* The decade culminated in the 1950 publication of *The Liberal Imagination,* a collection of the major essays written during that fertile period.

Even by the beginning of that decade Trilling had achieved considerable recognition. *Matthew Arnold* was widely and favorably reviewed and marked his emergence as a critic of national and international reputation. In March 1940 John Crowe Ransom was wooing him to *Kenyon Review:* "We want to publish very frequently from Lionel Trilling, for perfectly selfish reasons. . . . Please consider us a very immediate market." And in July Ransom assured him that he was "needed and wanted, *very much.*" Two years later, when the advisory board was reorganized, Ransom wrote, "Of course we have you down as No. 1 or anchor man on our Advisory Board," which included Cleanth Brooks and Robert Penn Warren.[74] Near the end of the forties, Trilling, along with Ransom and F. O. Matthiessen, founded the Kenyon School of Letters at Kenyon College in Gambier, Ohio—later to become the Indiana University School of Letters. He served as a senior fellow for this summer school when its visiting faculty included such people as R. P. Blackmur, Eric Bentley, Cleanth Brooks, Richard Chase, Allen Tate, William Empson, Alfred Kazin, Robert Lowell, Philip Rahv, René Wellek, Kenneth Burke, Robert Penn Warren, Austin Warren, Basil Willey, Yvor Winters, Newton Arvin, and Mark Schorer—a remarkable clustering of the most brilliant critics of the time.

In 1942, *Time* magazine was considering a new review policy with signed reviews by a house reviewer. Trilling was offered the job. "The offer came," he wrote Barzun, "through the astonishing Whittaker Chambers and his advice was 'Don't take it.' "[75] He did not take it, not because of Chambers's advice, but because it was a demanding full-time job that would have meant giving up teaching. He was tempted, he said, by the prospect that attracts most academics: the chance "of being in something real." On this occasion as well as on others, he no doubt contemplated earning his living exclusively by writing, as other New York intellectuals did, but he considered teaching as more than a "crutch." He once stated that for the writing of criticism, at least, "it seems invaluable to have to deal, on the one hand, with freshmen who are relatively intelligent but either ignorant of literature, or naive about it or even inimical to it, for it forcibly reminds the critic how small a part literature plays in our world and it makes him bring his assumptions out of their professional cave; then, on the other hand, it is very salutary to have to face talented seniors who will give one no quarter; and the subject matter, the most interesting work of the past, is always a refreshment" (*SLS,* 121).

One reason Ransom recruited Trilling for *Kenyon Review* was that he wanted representation from the New York writers—the New York intellectuals, as they have come to be known. The New York intellectuals connoted something faintly alien to our native American roots and national habits. Many were Jewish, from immigrant homes, nurtured in European radicalism. Irving Howe says they constituted "the first intelligentsia in American history—which is a shade different from a group of intellectuals." He makes the distinction on the basis of Renato Poggioli's definition of intelligentsia: "an intellectual order *from the lower ranks* . . . an intellectual order whose function was not so much cultural as political." The appearance of these New York writers in the thirties, says Howe, should be seen not just as "a rude, alien intrusion" but also as a step in the Europeanizing of American culture. They attempted to capture the idea of Europe for America: "That meant above all the idea of *another* culture, an older culture, one richer in moral possibilities, steeped in bloodier experiences, and closer to the tragic than ours could ever be."[76] The memoirs of members of this group all reveal that among them passion was in great abundance but manners in short supply. William Phillips, longtime editor of *Partisan Review,* describes it as "a brawling community, everyone trying to impose his views on everyone else by sheer force of logic and rhetoric, which was often merciless. We had not yet learned the academic mode of ignoring or accommodating to ideas we found repugnant." He characterizes New York intellectuals as "an articulate, polemical, politicized generation that came from nowhere and had as much trouble handling its success as its alienation. Though we thought of ourselves as dissidents, we always complained that we were not sufficiently heard and understood, even when we were having our greatest influence."[77]

The New York intellectuals have centered their publishing in *New Republic, Nation, Commentary, New York Review of Books,* and other leftist, anticommunist, partly political magazines, and most importantly in *Partisan Review.* Through the late thirties and early forties, Trilling found the stance of *Partisan Review* compatible with his own—a separation of politics and literature, yet not a complete separation: politics in a philosophical sense was relevant to literature. In 1937, Philip Rahv and William Phillips, the editors of *Partisan Review,* declared their independence from the Communist Party and voiced an aim to use Marxism as an instrument of analysis and evaluation. Later, in 1942, they turned away from the Marxist dialectic in favor of psychoanalytic explanations. This paralleled Trilling's increasing interest in Freud. He contributed frequently to *Partisan,* wrote the introduction to *The Partisan Reader* (1946), joined the advisory board in 1948, and, according to Diana Trilling, was at one time considered the heir apparent to the editorship.[78]

Some view Trilling as the representative New York intellectual. Grant Webster, for example, in his study of postwar American literary criticism, claims that in his essays, his novel, and his person, Trilling expressed "the intellectual and emotional dialectic of all the Intellectuals." Almost every move of the intellectuals, he asserts, was first made by Trilling, who served as "the Intellectuals' consciousness, or as Kazin puts it, as 'an Emersonian teacher of the Tribe.' "[79] In the eyes of David Daiches, Trilling was the perfect New York intellectual: "Intelligent, curious, humane, well read, interested in ideas, fascinated by other times and places, and immensely knowledgeable about European culture, he is at the same time metropolitan (with the provincialism that goes with true metropolitanism), self-conscious and professional in the practice of literary criticism, very much the *observer* of the great stream of American life that goes on around him, the sophisticated urban observer who is proud of the fact that his observation is undoctrinaire and untainted with snobbism."[80]

As typical of the New York intellectuals as Trilling might seem, considering him as their representative man is problematical, and not simply because that group, like any other, is much more diverse than stereotyping characterizations allow. In reality, Trilling was atypical in very significant ways. For example, he was an academic; most of the intellectuals were suspicious of academia. His grace, courtesy, and generosity (many called it sweetness) contrasted sharply with the brassy manners of many of his colleagues. He was neither leftist nor politicized to the degree other of these intellectuals were. His particular moral approach to literature was unique even in that morally fervent intellectual environment. He was always troubled by the marriage of Marxism and modernism that was such a fundamental assumption of the group associated with *Partisan*. And this list of anomalies could easily be expanded. William Chace is correct in noting that "Trilling, a New Yorker and a Jew, was nevertheless not wholly of his time or of his place."[81]

During the fifties he published two collections of essays, *The Opposing Self* and *A Gathering of Fugitives,* the latter consisting mainly of pieces written for the *Griffin* (succeeded by the *Mid-Century Review*), the monthly magazine of the Reader's Subscription Book Club, on whose selection board he served with Jacques Barzun and W. H. Auden from 1951 to 1963. He was elected to the National Institute of Arts and Letters in 1951 and selected as a fellow of the American Academy of Arts and Sciences the following year. In 1955 he was the first layman ever invited to give the Freud Anniversary Lecture before the New York Psychoanalytical Society. The lecture was published that year as *Freud and the Crisis of Our Culture* and later included in *Beyond Culture* as "Freud: Within and Beyond Culture." During most of this decade, probably the apex of his reputation, his name was rarely mentioned in print without admiration or at least great respect, but in the late fifties he was sniped at and sometimes roundly attacked. In a 1959 letter to a former student, he says that the condition of his reputation is such that "it is precisely the mark of an intellectual to find fault with what I say. There was a moment, a few years ago, when I was sacrosanct, but it has (happily) passed."[82]

Those who found fault with his work during the last fifteen years of his life were mainly those interested in critical theory. This was inevitable because the trends in literary study and criticism during that time moved steadily and rapidly away from the moral-cultural approach to which he was devoted. He says himself in the 1970 essay "What is Criticism?," the introduction to his *Literary Criticism: An Introductory Reader,* "At the present time the idea that literature is to be judged by its moral effect has virtually no place in critical theory." But he immediately adds, "In actual critical practice, however, it has a quite considerable vitality" (*LD,* 67). This statement throws light upon his own reputation since the sixties. Those aligned with the recent transforming influx of theory into American criticism—phenomenology, structuralism, poststructuralism, radically antimimetic aesthetics—are likely to find Trilling old-fashioned in his insistence that literature is a criticism of life, irrelevant in his indifference to theory, quaint in his moral preoccupations, and tiresome in his suspicion of the new. Meanwhile, among the much larger group of readers and teachers of literature, those either uninitiated into the mysteries of recent critical theory or repelled by them, Trilling's devoted attention to the interrelationship of literature and life, art and conduct, seems appropriate, unavoidable, and illuminating.

Between 1960 and 1975, his increasing uneasiness with the modern temper found expression in *Beyond Culture: Essays on Learning and Literature* (1965), *Sincerity and Authenticity* (1972, based on the Charles Eliot Norton lectures delivered at Harvard in 1969–70), and *Mind in the Modern World* (1972, a lecture given upon receiving the National Endowment for the Humanities' first Thomas Jefferson Award). His lasting commitment to teaching was reflected in his editing of *The Experience of Literature* (1967, an anthology with extensive critical commentary) and *Literary Criticism: An Introductory Reader* (1970), and his coediting of *The Oxford Anthology of English Literature.* His profound admiration for Freud resulted in his editing with Steven Marcus an abridgment of Ernest Jones's three-volume *The Life and Work of Sigmund Freud* (1970). His achievement was recognized in visiting lectureships at Harvard and Oxford, a Creative Arts Award from Brandeis, and honorary degrees from Harvard, Northwestern, Case Western Reserve, Brandeis, and Yale universities in the United States and the universities of Durham and Leicester in England. When he died of cancer in 1975, he was working under a Guggenheim Fellowship.

Chapter Two
Arnold and Forster

Why Matthew Arnold?

Trilling explains in his autobiographical notes that when he undertook his study of Matthew Arnold he had no desire to become a scholar, but having chosen teaching as a profession, he needed a Ph.D. to establish himself. This required writing a dissertation, which at Columbia at the time meant a published book. He describes his selection of Arnold for a subject as having been a rather arbitrary choice. All he knew about Arnold derived from his especially personal response to the melancholy of some of the poems. "I thought it would be interesting to discover and explain in historical-cultural terms why he was so sad." Beginning with the melancholy poet who passively suffered "the stresses and tendencies of his culture," Trilling eventually became interested in "the man who had pitted himself against the culture, who had tried to understand the culture for the purpose of shaping it—with the critic, with (perhaps it can be said) the first literary intellectual in the English-speaking world" (*LD,* 238–39).

The reasons for his choosing to study Arnold may be less arbitrary than these statements indicate. The phrase "to discover and explain in historical-cultural terms" suggests a prior orientation, the thought of Marx and Freud. From them he got "the sense of the actuality and intimacy of history, of society, of culture" and the felt necessity "of discovering the causative principles of these entities." It was these concerns, he says, that "controlled" his study of Arnold (*LD,* 237). It is also possible that his choice of Arnold was determined to some extent by the rising interest in humanism in the late twenties and early thirties, during which time a number of influential books examining various aspects of humanism were published. The controversy over the "New Humanism" fostered by Irving Babbitt and Paul Elmer More came to a head in 1930 with the publication of *Humanism and America: Essays on the Outlook of Modern Civilization,* edited by Norman Foerster, and *The Critique of Humanism: A Symposium,* edited by C. Hartley Grattan. The humanistic tradition, of which Arnold was a leading representative, was at the center of literary-intellectual discussion just at the time Trilling was searching for a dissertation topic. That he was aware of this discussion is evidenced by the references to Babbitt and More in *Matthew Arnold.* But it was not to contemporary American humanists that he was drawn; his close intellectual and scholarly ties to the English and European literary traditions channeled his interest toward Arnold himself and the European writers to whom Arnold was indebted.

Whatever the reasons behind it, Trilling's choice of Arnold as the subject for his first ambitious critical undertaking was uncannily apt and remarkably fraught with consequences. In Arnold he found confirmation and reinforcement for many of his own interests and predispositions. His propensity for ambivalence, his taste for subtlety, and his willingness to wrestle with complexity found nurture in Arnold's similar qualities. Responding to the literary-intellectual currents of the late twenties and early thirties, he recognized "that the culture of humanism was at a point of crisis" and that "the society which had sustained this culture was in dire straits" (*LD,* 235). Arnold, he discovered, had struggled with a similar crisis in society and culture and had illuminated many of its fundamental issues. Arnold's conception of literature as a criticism of life, as an instrument of the best kind of education, coincided with Trilling's own strong convictions about the function of literature, and particularly the novel. For example, he expressed those convictions to Barzun in 1938: "I must start reading novels again. I forget that from them I got all the education I have; they make a better man of me, which books of philosophycriticismhistory do not."[1] It is difficult to imagine that he could have found a more congenial and generative topic for his dissertation. He confined to Barzun in 1937 that the Arnold book "has gotten so much more important than a book like this ought to be: it seems to me that I have been recording my education in it for five or six years."[2]

His early and extensive study of Arnold, furthermore, had consequences far beyond the personal. Though he resolved at the book's completion to put Arnold out of his mind, having no desire to be known as "an Arnold man," Arnold remained for him a lifetime mentor. During the forties, he says in the autobiographical notes, "I found myself confronting a situation that I had inevitably to understand in Arnold's own terms" (*LD,* 239). Though calling himself a liberal, Arnold had devoted his major effort in criticism to questioning the assumptions and reasonings of liberal thought. Trilling found himself enlisted in the same undertaking. In short, the influential reevaluation of liberalism during the forties and fifties, for which Trilling is famous, was determined by his study of Arnold. Moreover, that effort, along with his criticism in general, perpetuated into our century the long critical tradition that Arnold represented, a tradition of discriminators between the false and true, the deformed and sound; preachers of harmony and proportion and order; prophets of the religion of taste. If this tradition has dealt much with literature it is because there it finds life displayed in its infinitely varied motives and results; its practice has always been to render literature itself more consciously a criticism of life. Trilling kept this tradition alive in a century whose prevailing literary and critical fashions have ignored or discredited it.

Questions about how and for whom one should write and about the distinctions between criticism and scholarship characterized the intellectual temper of the late twenties and early thirties. Responding to this temper, Trilling set out deliberately to write a book that "should find its audience not among scholars but among the general public," a work of criticism, not of scholarship. The distinction was significant then; in fact, one of his examiners said sternly that what he had presented was no doubt a good *book* but was by no means a good *dissertation* (*LD,* 238–39). Despite Trilling's acknowledged intention, *Matthew Arnold* is better suited if not to scholars then to a reasonably literate audience than to the general public, at least today's general public. It assumes acquaintance with Arnold and is not a how-to-know-Arnold book. It also assumes some acquaintance with nineteenth-century English history and with a considerable smattering of European philosophy. And although the style is lucid and readable, it has a certain scholarly stiffness that Trilling put aside in his subsequent writing.

The book has been highly successful. It was reviewed widely and positively in the major periodicals of the day and has remained in print for most of the years since its publication. In his review for the *New Republic,* Edmund Wilson said Trilling had written "one of the first critical studies of any solidity and scope by an American of his generation."[3] In England Edward Sackville-West acclaimed it as "the most brilliant piece of biographical criticism issued in English during the last ten years."[4] Before it actually appeared, Barzun, who had read the chapters as Trilling wrote them, said, "You have written a magnum opus and that's that."[5]

Arnold and the Nineteenth Century

Trilling's purpose as stated in his introduction was "to show the thought of Matthew Arnold in its complex unity and to relate it to the historical and intellectual events of his time." This study, he says, might be thought of as "a biography of Arnold's mind." In some ways the book is wider in scope than this statement of purpose suggests. As one reviewer observed, "It comes very near to being a study of the mind of the nineteenth century, with Arnold as its focal point."[6] The reader who comes to the book seeking specific biographical information or detailed explications of Arnold's poems will be disappointed. *Matthew Arnold* was published before extensive biographical information was available, and Trilling explains that he consulted almost no unpublished material and used biographical matter only incidentally to his critical purpose. He was as much interested in the age as in Arnold and his focus constantly shifts from one to the other. The book does what Arnold said in his essay on Heine that criticism should do—place the subject in the age's main current of ideas. And Trilling's treatment of the poetry as well as the prose manifests this central concern with historical-philosophical context.

Trilling's original intention of investigating the historical-cultural causes of the sadness in Arnold's poetry determined his starting point and constitutes the orienting thrust of the first chapter. From there he launches into historical-political-cultural backgrounds, beginning with a chapter on "His Father and His England." The essential pattern of the book from this point on parallels the evolution of Arnold's career from poetry to literary criticism to politics and finally to religion. Trilling portrays each stage of Arnold's interests and activities as growing with a striking logicality out of the one before. And it is this essential unity of Arnold's thought despite his diverse interests and undertakings that engaged Trilling's interest and provided his central thesis. It also posed his central problem, which was to account for the transformation of a shy, melancholy poet, lamenting a lost peace in the midst of confusion, into the assertive critic of society and confident prophet of culture. Trilling's ultimate answer is that the poet's vision gave the prose writer his goal: Arnold the poet first saw the problems that Arnold the practical man tried to solve. Melancholy generated his best poems, and when he turned to cheerfulness he turned to prose, the transformation being brought about by his personal need for affirmation.

In the preface to the second edition, Trilling agrees with the reviewers who said that he had not paid enough attention to the aesthetics of Arnold's poetry. It is obvious in "The Making of Myths," the chapter on poetry, that his concern is with ideas rather than aesthetics. Such things as rhythm, images, meter, form, metaphor are scarcely mentioned. Instead we find frequent mention of the philosophical ideas of Carlyle, Mill, Coleridge, Kant, Spinoza, Fichte, Burke, Godwin, and others. This sentence is typical: "The loneliness which Arnold represents in the person of Empedocles is no small part of the burden of his age" (*MA,* 111). Such a topic sentence is obviously going to generate discussion of content rather than form, politics rather than prosody. And when Trilling says that "not all of Arnold's more explicitly philosophical poetry can give us so clear an insight into his feelings about the cosmos and society as can his poems of sexual love" (*MA,* 122), we recognize that even the love poems are going to be examined more for their social ideas than for their beauty. His admission to slighting the aesthetic can hardly be interpreted as repentant, for never in his subsequent career did he engage in extensive aesthetic analysis. He was more comfortable with prose than poetry, and although capable of sensitive close reading, he treated artistic technique primarily as a means of conveying ideas or emotional attitudes that could be translated into ideas.

The book faintly resembles an encyclopedia of nineteenth-century intellectual and social history. It provides, among much historical information, an account of the rise of the middle class with its laissez-faire policy, the conflict between the Anglican church and the dissenting bodies, the decay of Bible Christianity and the attempt to dissociate the Christian idea from dogma, and the cropping up of theories of race. Trilling displays a marked proclivity for backgrounds. Before examining Matthew Arnold, he provides a biography of Thomas Arnold, including such detail as the specific policies and objectives of his school, Rugby. When he treats Matthew Arnold's work as a school inspector, he feels obliged to provide detailed information about the history and politics of education in England. When he points out how Coleridge's ideas on the Bible influenced Arnold, he feels the necessity of backing up to Spinoza's influence on Coleridge. Indeed, the book is filled with references to such continental authors as Goethe, Balzac, Stendhal, Musset, Saint-Beuve, Chateaubriand, and Leopardi. Such information is useful and interesting, but by constantly backing up so far in considering the context of Arnold's thought, Trilling runs the risk of blurring the focus on Arnold himself.

Some reviewers suggested that he included too much. Edmund Wilson observed that although nothing is said of Arnold's wife, the Victorian supercrank Francis Newman is re-created. Another reviewer questioned the necessity of the long synopsis of *Robert Elsmere,* a novel written by Arnold's niece. W. S. Knickerbocker delineated three books in *Matthew Arnold:* (1) what aspires to be a biography of Arnold's mind; (2) miscellaneous interruptions—"like corpses lugged from behind the arras"—of expository explanations of great thinkers supposed to have influenced Arnold: Vico, Spinoza, Saint Paul, Goethe, Plato, Bishop Colenso, Burke, Bishop Butler, and Kant; and (3) "an instructive, edifying, and occasionally stodgy revelation of Mr. Lionel Trilling's own solutions of our present difficulties and his corrections of Matthew Arnold's deficiencies."[7]

Despite such strictures, the book, taken in the terms of its own conception, remains a brilliant and comprehensive achievement—in C. F. Harrold's words, "an extremely helpful attempt to place Arnold not only in the pattern of the nineteenth century but also in the whole modern tradition, from the Renaissance to T. S. Eliot and I. A. Richards, and Marx and Freud."[8]

Principal Themes in *Matthew Arnold*

The contours of Trilling's treatment of Arnold, and of his admiration for him, are essentially encompassed in four principal themes or characteristics.

One is Arnold's tendency to view literature ultimately in a social perspective. The key to Arnold's whole position as a critic, says Trilling, is that he "is concerned not merely with the nature and quality of the work under consideration but also with the effect of the work upon the reader and, eventually, upon the polity" (*MA,* 428). According to Trilling, the spiritual disease Arnold grappled with in his poetry was "one of the inevitabilities of a social organization in which the wisdom of society can no longer be accepted: put the burden of ethical judgment entirely upon the individual, make him accept the rightness of the Kantian imperative and almost certainly, unless he is insensitively arrogant, he will end in doubt and inaction" (*MA,* 130). Here is the problem of the relationship between the self and society. Trilling found it at the center of Arnold's thought, and it became a central and enduring concern of his own. As Arnold moved from poetry to prose in his search for affirmation, Trilling explains, he was brought to the definite and the actual—to society in its ever-changing forms. He began "to think of the social and political determination of literature and the need for social and political reorganization." Behind every critical judgment of literature that Arnold would henceforth make "lies a social and political judgment" (*MA,* 159). Even when he is talking about style, "he is talking about society" (*MA,* 166). The "great truth" that he would keep ever before him and develop with increasing explicitness, says Trilling, "is that all human values, all human emotions, are of social growth if not of social origin. . . . Understanding what the human individual must do for himself, Arnold knows how much of what man does for himself depends upon what society allows him to do. He is clear—and grows clearer—about the cause of human isolation and the sterilization of the emotions. He knows it is not merely a religious problem—though that too—but a social problem" (*MA,* 113). This "great truth" that Trilling found so primary in Arnold became his own great concern and accounts for his later fascination with Freud's treatment of it in *Civilization and Its Discontents.*

The Portable Matthew Arnold, published ten years after *Matthew Arnold,* displays this same emphasis on society. Trilling defines Arnold's humanism there in specifically social terms as "the attitude of those men who think it an advantage to live in society, and, at that, in a complex and highly developed society, and who believe that man fulfills his nature and reaches his proper stature in this circumstance." Humanism cherishes the personal virtues of "intelligence, amenity, and tolerance" and the courage that supports these virtues. "The qualities of intelligence which it chiefly prizes are modulation and flexibility—it wants the mind to be, in the words of Montaigne which Arnold admired, *ondoyant et divers,*" that is, undulating and diverse (*PMA,* 3). Clearly, the humanism Trilling attributes to Arnold and which received his own firm allegiance is based on the quest for a properly balanced relationship between individual and society.

A second Arnoldian theme that evokes Trilling's special interest and sympathy is disinterestedness, the kind of objectivity that curbs the impulse to immediate action in favor of critical observation and thinking that gradually—over the long term—produce sounder change. As Arnold expresses the idea in "Stanzas in Memory of the Author of 'Obermann,' " "He who hath watch'd, not shared, the strife, / Knows how the day hath gone." Perhaps recoiling from the activism of the thirties, Trilling concurred with Arnold's explicit admonition that the poet must give up action if he is to live his true life, no matter how socially useful the action may be. As for the philosophical man, he too must be, in Arnold's words, "to men's business not too near"; he must not, says Trilling, "expect action to answer doubts, though it may quiet them" (*MA,* 101). The task of literature, Trilling agreed with Arnold, is to promote civilization by making men more reasonable, social, spiritually enlightened, morally sensitive, and clear thinking—able "to see the object as in itself it really is." When Arnold referred to poetry as a criticism of life, says Trilling, he was stating the function of poetry: "Criticism is not what poetry *is;* it is what poetry *does*" (*MA,* 196). Trilling defends Arnold's theory of literature, saying it is not the product of the ivory tower or an incapacity to act. "It implies that true art can settle no questions, give no directives; that it can do no more than cultivate what is best in the reader—his moral poise." But rather than being an escape from the conditions of modern life, true art "seeks to send men back into daily living with spirits restored" (*MA,* 152–53). According to Trilling, Arnold discounted action not because he had a quarrel with action itself, but because he knew "that it goes beyond itself, becomes a means of faith, a way of escaping thought and what seems to be the humiliations of necessary doubt" (*MA,* 8–9). Elsewhere, Trilling seems to confront the dilemma of action versus disinterestedness by suggesting that the latter is itself a form of positive action: "To discover and define, then, the dominant tendency of his age, to analyze the good from the bad, foster the good, diminish the bad—this will be Arnold's program of criticism. Its keynote is activism and affirmation: objectivity, in short" (*MA,* 159–60). It may seem odd to equate objectivity with activism and affirmation, but Trilling believed that a distorting subjectivity comes so naturally to humankind that assertive effort is required to resist it. This belief helps account for his own tendency to take a middle position, which has often been interpreted by his critics as passivity or mere indecision.

Trilling found the key to Arnold's importance and to his method of disinterestedness in this statement he made about criticism: "It must be apt to study and praise elements that for the fulness of spiritual perfection are wanted, even though they belong to a power which in the practical sphere may be maleficent. It must be apt to discern the spiritual shortcomings or illusions of powers that in the practical sphere may be beneficent" (*MA,* 205). This ideal of objectivity elicited Trilling's greatest respect.

A third theme to which Trilling responds often and profoundly is Arnold's notion of culture as a process largely governed by reason but not restricted to the rational intellect alone, a process that enlists the whole of human faculties. If we follow the fluctuations and sometimes confusing modulations of Arnold's thought, says Trilling, we will find that his criticism seeks a reconciliation of rationalism and faith. "He steers a course both by compass and by stars: reason, but not the cold and formal reason that makes the mind a machine; faith, but not the escape from earth-binding facts. 'The main element of the modern spirit's life,' he says, 'is neither the senses and understanding, nor the heart and imagination; it is the imaginative reason.' " We must understand this notion of imaginative reason, insists Trilling, in order to understand how literature is a criticism of life and an agent of culture (*MA,* 194). "Culture," he says, "is not merely a method but an attitude of spirit contrived to receive truth. It is a moral orientation, involving will, imagination, faith; all of these avowedly active elements body forth a universe that contains a truth which the intuition can grasp and the analytical reason can scrutinize. Culture is reason involving the whole personality; it is the whole personality in search of the truth" (*MA,* 265). Trilling reiterated this interpretation of Arnold's concept of culture in a 1954 introduction to Arnold, which is included in the Uniform Edition of *Matthew Arnold:* "culture is that totality of the imaginative reason which must be applied to our social and political life if anarchy is not to prevail" (*MA,* 429).

He says that for Arnold, "the dominance of the rational intellect, the loss of the old intuitive knowledge, is the sign of the aging and decay not merely of the individual but of the whole culture" (*MA,* 424). This recognition of the limits of rational intellect struck a responsive chord in Trilling, who believed that to face everything with the intellect is to be unanchored to the earth. "And worse yet: the intellect, pushed into this new dominance, may displace emotion and check the warm and simple flow of natural life." He interpreted Arnold's "The Scholar Gypsy" as "a passionate indictment of the new dictatorship of the never-resting intellect over the soul of modern man" (*MA,* 112). Arnold's belief that society is of so organic a nature that it prohibits the interference of the analytical intellect and his consequent hostility to system-makers were forceful influences upon Trilling in his criticism of liberalism's tendency toward rationalistic programs, toward idealistic conceptions that ignore actual human nature and experience.

The fourth theme or characteristic that Trilling emphasized because it coincided with his own temperament or mental disposition was what he called Arnold's "historical and dialectical" method. He admired

Arnold's tendency to take into account historical circumstances as he mediated between extremes and shunned absolutes. Trilling accepted this sort of dialectical way of thinking in place of the Marxist version. He says that Arnold rejected historical criticism based on the "scientific" assumption that thorough knowledge of historical context inevitably provides complete knowledge of the individual writer. Instead, Arnold "always insisted that the act of criticism requires that we suspend our absolute standards and look at events or ideas, whether past or present, in the light of their historical determinants." Arnold's judgment of the French Revolution exemplifies his method at work. "Was he a partisan of the Revolution or its vigorous opponent? We might show by quotation that he was either or both, but actually he was neither; his feeling about the Revolution was determined, first, by his notion of the historical context in which it had occurred and, second, by the particular historical moment in which he was writing" (*MA,* 6). A second example is the way Arnold held in suspension a "stringent materialistic naturalism" and "the Platonic—or 'realist' position." "He did not struggle between the two views and in a sense they did not produce any fundamental contradiction, as they would have had he attempted a systematic philosophy. He allowed them to exist side by side; each was used to mitigate what Arnold thought were the excesses of the other in modern life" (*MA,* 94–95).

The one "critical lesson" that Arnold never ceased to teach, says Trilling, was that history "must be considered neutrally—and dialectically." At the risk of seeming to call Arnold a Marxist, he quotes a long passage by Engels on the dialectical process, which asserts that what now seems true has its latent false side and what seems false has its latent true side. He then comments that "the ambivalence of opinion which the dialectical method produces is an impossible burden to some people but to others it is a positive pleasure; Arnold was one of the latter" (*MA,* 180). And, of course, so was Trilling.

Manifesting the influence of his own historical moment, the thirties, Trilling says Arnold's "subtle dialectic" tends to be misrepresented in a world "where action presses and where it is believed that the coexistence of two ideas must keep us from acting on either" (*MA,* 5). In the second preface (1949), he again voices his concern about our loss of the sense of human limits, powers, and processes, "of our turning to the desperate absolute." As an example and corrective, he places the poise and moderation of Arnold's dialectical method in direct opposition to the doctrinal rigidity and programmatic intolerance of the modern intelligence. Our liberals and intellectuals, he says, are "even less eager than ten years ago to see the object as it really is, less willing to believe that in a time of change and danger openness and flexibility of mind are, as Arnold said, the first virtues."

Arnold's Influence on Trilling

Arnold exerted an extremely fertilizing influence on Trilling, the kind that generates kinship and deep affinity. From our standpoint, it is difficult if not impossible to read *Matthew Arnold* without having the sense that Trilling was unconsciously charting the course of his own intellectual life in writing about Arnold's. In light of his subsequent career, many of the concerns, ideas, and values expressed in this book constitute a portrait of Trilling's own mind as much as of Arnold's. In fact, the many similarities tempt us, as Jacques Barzun warns, to view Trilling's career as simply a continuation of Arnold's work. "Arnold's purpose is mainly a moral purpose," says Barzun. "Trilling's is political and intellectual—and moral in a different sense."[9] Trilling's disagreements with Arnold of course need to be recognized. For example, although he shared Arnold's concern with the well-being of society, he focused more on the complexity of human relationships within it. This led to differences from Arnold in which he found arguments and emphases more fitted to his own interests and experience. Arnold stressed that the effect of great literature should culminate in action. Trilling, influenced by Freud, felt that the moral effect of literature may also be realized in a beneficial lessening of stress or rigidity or in an increased freedom from compulsive behavior. Obviously, Trilling was only mildly sympathetic with Arnold's religious affirmations, and he was openly skeptical about his confidence in the possibilities of a powerful and beneficent state existing above class interests. He criticized Arnold's famous apology for the status quo drawn from Joubert's maxim, "Force until right is ready," and he disapproved of Arnold's theory of race expressed in his view of Celtic literature.

As such differences are recognized, it becomes clear that Trilling's inheritance from Arnold had more to do with qualities of mind and temperament than with specific doctrines, programs, or ideas. "It goes without saying," he says in the introduction, "that admiration for a writer does not mean agreement. Indeed, I believe it will be apparent that it is much more with Arnold's method that I am in agreement than with his conclusions" (*MA,* 10). Trilling found it of little consequence that Arnold was wrong on one point or another, or even on many points. He thought, in fact, that a critic who is essentially right "may be most interesting and most powerful and most useful when he is wrong, that his mistakes may sometimes be the most vital part of him, for they represent his passion and commitment" (*MA,* 409). If a critic is worth reading, he will make mistakes "because he has in mind something besides his perceptions about art in itself—he has in mind the demands he makes upon life; and those critics are most to be trusted who allow these demands, in all their particularity, to be detected by their readers." Arnold's mistakes are in the open, but "so are the lively principles by which he made them." It is not necessary to agree with Arnold's conclusions to enjoy and benefit from his criticism: "It is only necessary to be aware of the generosity and commitment of his enterprise" (*PMA,* 184).

But even when the debt to Arnold is qualified, the fact remains that a man is known by the tradition with which he identifies himself, and Trilling clearly identified himself with the tradition Arnold represented and advanced. Arnold's conception of criticism obviously shaped Trilling's own ideas of the proper task of the critic and legitimized his preoccupation with social and cultural matters. Like Arnold he was prompted to discover absolutes that underlie the fluctuations of time, place, and customs. Like Arnold he believed persons fulfill their highest potential in society. Like Arnold he had a heightened awareness of complexity in human affairs and yet a simultaneous respect for individuals' limited but real capacity to influence their own destiny. Like Arnold he was intensely interested in class and its conditioning power. Like Arnold he was most interested in the middle class because of its intellectual potential. Perhaps what links him to Arnold more than anything else is his overweening concern with morality. For both, literature's basis of value is that it has a moral effect.

After acknowledging the differences between Arnold and Trilling, John Henry Raleigh lists seven fundamental resemblances: (1) They both, in reaction to the provinciality of their culture, sought sustenance in European thinkers. Arnold turned to the French critics, Goethe, and Spinoza; Trilling to Freud, Hegel, and Rousseau. (2) Neither devoted much attention to literary contemporaries; both were more concerned with applying great literature of the past to an interpretation of present cultural realities and the disorientation of modern societies. (3) Both used the romantics (Trilling added the Victorians) as a usable tradition from which to examine modern life and culture. (4) Each viewed the modern condition as the product of the tension between the rational ideology of the French Revolution and the emotional complexities of the romantic self. (5) Both recognized the tragic nature of the human condition—for Arnold, because one world was dead and the other unborn, and for Trilling because of the implications of Freud's *Civilization and Its Discontents.* Modern civilization has brought losses—religious for Arnold, literary for Trilling. For both, the stay against anarchy and confusion is culture and the critical self in a posture of vigilance. (6) Though the human condition is tragic and modern society is in disarray, both found enduring values not in abstractions but in the potential abilities of persons to discover their own inner strengths. What is needed is social conditions that allow that self-discovery. (7) Both held the same view of the function of the critic: to stand at what Trilling called the "dark and bloody crossroad" of literature and politics, harrying simple-minded friends and hoping for usefully challenging arguments from enemies, practicing a "disinterestedness" that is not a disengagement from experience but the connecting of ideas and experience.[10] When Trilling emerged from his long initial encounter with Matthew Arnold, his critical attitudes, values, and predispositions were firmly established, and he had achieved a wide and respected reputation.

From Arnold to Forster

At first glance, *E. M. Forster,* published in 1943, appears to be quite different from *Matthew Arnold.* It is much shorter and, with chapters devoted to particular novels, presents itself as being more strictly literary criticism than biography or intellectual and cultural history. But closer inspection reveals clear threads of continuity in themes and method running through both books. While writing on Arnold, Trilling had been reading Forster's fiction and responding to it from an Arnoldian perspective. The two authors came together in his mind as allies in their application of dialectical intelligence to the critique of liberalism. "Forster's manner," says Trilling, "is the agent of a moral intention which can only be carried out by the mind *ondoyant et divers* of which Montaigne spoke" (*EMF,* 5). Trilling, of course, learned this ideal of the undulating and diverse mind from Arnold, who was fond of quoting Montaigne's phrase. If Trilling acquired most of his education from novels, as he said he did, he must have learned a good deal from Forster, and what he learned was conditioned by or filtered through his study of Arnold. Consequently, *E. M. Forster* is, to a significant extent, a continuation or extension of *Matthew Arnold,* in which Forster's fiction is portrayed as expressing, among other ideas and attitudes, the four themes mentioned above as being fundamental to Trilling's response to Arnold: the relationship of self to society, the value of disinterestedness or the relaxed will, the dangers of overweening intellect, and the necessity of a dialectical disposition of mind.

Moreover, Trilling's method in *E. M. Forster* resembles that used in *Matthew Arnold* more than might at first be apparent. Although the former is a critical study of particular literary works, it is more than literary analysis and more than a book on Forster. Like the Arnold book, it often dwells upon social, political, and cultural issues. Morton Dauwen Zabel describes it as "an examination of the conscience of contemporary literature and thinking."[11] It contains a substantial amount of literary analysis, but, more important, it contains Trilling's digressions on matters only incidentally connected with Forster, digressions on the nature of plot, comedy, tragedy, and criticism and on class conflict, moral vision, and the weaknesses of liberalism. As with the Arnold book, readers have complained of a paucity of aesthetic judgments. David Daiches, after praising the book, remarks that Trilling "is too often content with extracting, explaining and criticizing the 'message' of the novels, and letting the result stand as a literary judgment."[12] E. B. Greenwood complains that Trilling never really dealt with Forster from the standpoint of literary criticism: "He remained a critic of ideas throughout."[13]

In the preface to the second edition (1964), Trilling acknowledges his ulterior purposes in writing the book, explaining that it was written in a concentrated rush. Much of the enthusiasm and pleasure in the writing were due to his liking for the subject, but he admits to having benefited "by the special energies that attend a polemical purpose" (*EMF,* ix). The book was intended as a corrective to things liberal and things American. William M. Chace suggests that "it is not so much written as aimed."[14] "I had a quarrel with American literature as at that time it was established," says Trilling, "and against what seemed to me its dullness and its pious social simplicities I enlisted Mr. Forster's vivacity, complexity, and irony" (*EMF,* ix). It was a quarrel that was to occupy him for some years. From the title of the first chapter of this study of Forster, he took the name of his first collection of essays, *The Liberal Imagination,* which was a forceful continuation of the quarrel. *E. M. Forster* is of particular interest for the directness with which it sets forth the normative principles Trilling used to critique liberalism. He used Forster as a sort of touchstone. Therefore, having been oriented in his critical posture by his study of Arnold, Trilling enlisted Forster's "moral realism" and "dialectical intelligence" in his own formidable opposition to the unimaginative and oversimplifying pieties of his liberal contemporaries.

Forster and the Liberal Imagination

Trilling says Forster is the only living novelist he can read again and again and have "the sensation of having learned something" (*EMF,* 3). This statement provides a key to the book's prime conception; it is designed to show what can be learned from Forster's fiction, and the design has a certain urgency because what can be learned is a needed corrective to the current literary-intellectual tendencies Trilling finds alarming. Consequently, Trilling's criticism in this study is primarily thematic. Most of the chapters begin with an explicit statement of theme that constitutes a sort of thesis or topic for the chapter. Trilling's first love was the Victorian novel. He thought "the literary intelligence was prouder in those days and glittered more" (*EMF,* 39). He found Forster somewhat like those earlier novelists—concerned with ideas. And he admired him for taking "full and conscious responsibility for his novels, refusing to share in the increasingly dull assumption of the contemporary novelist that the writer has nothing to do with the story he tells" (*EMF,* 5). It is ideas that interest Trilling, and moral ideas in particular; "moral" appears as a frequent adjective in his discussion of Forster: moral essence, moral purpose, moral fiber, moral dimension, moral symbol, moral quality, moral intelligence. The penetrating treatment of ideas is the chief strength of the book and is characterized by an awareness of the dangers of treating ideas out of context: "To summarize any good, developed idea is to betray it; we must have not only its conclusions but its dialectical growth, and we must have its modifications" (*EMF,* 41).

It is Forster's appreciation of the dialectical growth and modification of ideas that Trilling most admires, and he warns that a mind unable to tolerate complication might be averse to Forster. "For he stands in a peculiar reaction to what, for want of a better word, we may call the liberal tradition, that loose body of middle-class opinion which includes such ideas as progress, collectivism and humanitarianism" (*EMF,* 7). Though long committed to liberalism, Forster "is at war with the liberal imagination." The weakness of this imagination, Trilling argues, is that it is always being surprised. "Liberalism likes to suggest its affinity with science, pragmatism and the method of hypothesis, but in actual conduct it requires 'ideals' and absolutes; it prefers to make its alliances only when it thinks it catches the scent of Utopia in parties and governments, the odor of sanctity in men; and if neither is actually present, liberalism makes sure to supply it." Because most human action diverges from the ideal and absolute, liberalism is always being surprised and affronted by actual human experience (*EMF,* 8), and despite its sweet attractions, it is incompetent in the face of complication, tragedy, and death. Moreover, the liberal is always investing in the future and discrediting the past and consequently does not appreciate the present. Forster, in Trilling's view, does not make these mistakes. He accepts "the human fact as we know it now" and is content with human possibilities and limitations. He is worldly in the sense of accepting man in the world "without the sentimentality of cynicism and without the sentimentality of rationalism" (*EMF,* 14–15). He is always tampering with the heroic, shocking us by undercutting the heroism of his heroes and heroines. It is "a kind of mithridate against our being surprised by life" (*EMF,* 11).

The lesson Trilling finds in Forster may be summed up in the term *moral realism,* a quality produced by the dialectical intelligence with its avoidance of oversimplification and absolutes. "All novelists deal with morality, but not all novelists, or even all good novelists, are concerned with moral realism, which is not the awareness of morality itself but of the contradictions, paradoxes, and dangers of living the moral life" (*EMF,* 6). Trilling places Forster in the line of Hawthorne and James in his understanding of the inextricable tangle of good and evil and of the perils of moral action. The moral realist sees the world not in terms of good and evil but good-and-evil, the hyphens suggesting the ineluctable mixture in human motivations. He is not surprised by life because he has weighed possibilities and alternatives and recognized and accepted limitations. Forster "refuses to be conclusive. No sooner does he come to a conclusion than he must unravel it again" (*EMF,* 10). Trilling is sympathetic with this ability to remain inconclusive and open to the possibility of further hypotheses, an ability he later links to negative capability in his essay on John Keats and alludes to repeatedly in the course of his writing.

Trilling thought the lesson of moral realism was particularly appropriate for liberalism. "Before the idea of good-and-evil its imagination fails; it cannot accept this improbable paradox." This is ironic, he adds, because one of the charter-documents of liberalism, Milton's *Areopagitica,* encourages the cultivation of imagination enough to accept just this improbability. After quoting the passage describing the way good and evil grow up inseparably in this world—"It was from out the rind of one apple tasted, that the knowledge of good and evil, as two twins cleaving together, leaped forth into the world"—he remarks how the irony is doubled by the fact that great conservative minds such as Johnson and Burke understood perfectly well what Milton meant, and Arnold was thought less liberal for his understanding of it. "But we of the liberal connection have always liked to play the old intellectual game of antagonistic principles. . . . Forster will not play this game; or, rather, he plays it only to mock it" (*EMF,* 8–9).

Like Arnold, Forster distrusted the intellect and its games. Untempered rationalism is the very thing that can disorient moral realism. "To Forster, who has so often spoken of the saving virtues of intellect, the intellect, which can be the source of life, can also, at certain intensities, be treacherous" (*EMF,* 131). In tracing the evolution of the intellectual, Trilling explains that the intensity and rigidity of the intellect as a rarified power are often accompanied by self-righteousness: "Consequently, liberal intellectuals have always moved in an aura of self-congratulation. They sustain themselves by flattering themselves with intentions and they dismiss as 'reactionary' whoever questions them. When the liberal intellectual thinks of himself, he thinks chiefly of his own good will and prefers not to know that the good will generates its own problems, that the love of humanity has its own vices and the love of truth its own insensibilities. The choice of the moral course does not settle the quality of morality" (*EMF,* 92).

In light of these dangers inherent in the rational intellect, especially when combined with an energized will, Trilling suggests that "to retreat from the fierce sun of the intellect, to abandon the strictness of order and law may at certain times be the best means of asserting the intellect and order and law" (*EMF,* 132). Forster recognizes this paradox, and in his belief in "the relaxed will, in the deep suspiciousness of the rigid exercise of the intellect, there lies the deepest faith in the will and intellect" (*EMF,* 136). The recognized need to moderate will and intellect reflected here was fundamental in Trilling's development as a moral critic. He saw it as the vital ingredient in "the moral intelligence of art," which acts as a shield against the panic and emptiness that arise when the will and intellect are tired of their own excesses.

Trilling found Forster to be secular in an appealing way. In addition to the modulated rationalism just mentioned, Forster, though lacking faith in the regenerative power of Christianity and being frequently hostile to the clergy, displays "a tenderness for religion because it expresses, though it does not solve, the human mystery" (*EMF,* 12). This sense of being open to the irreducible complexity and mystery of human life produces a wholeness of vision that prevents reductionism. This vision recognizes man as being neither beast nor angel. Trilling describes Forster as "one of the thinking people who were never led by thought to suppose they could be more than human and who, in bad times, will not become less" (*EMF,* 16).

Being neither more nor less than human has important social implications, and Trilling sees Forster as always concerned with the private life in its public connection. In fact, he identifies Forster's uniqueness and intellectual heroism as being constituted by the way "he makes his private judgments under the aspect of the nation—or all the nations" (*EMF,* 23). Forster's great central theme, according to Trilling, was "the underdeveloped heart," that is, the untrained or untutored heart, which Forster saw as largely responsible for England's political problems. Trilling admired Forster's ability to portray the vital nexus between culture and character. His commentary on the novels calls attention to the way Forster gives the greatest reality to social forces. He suggests that Forster's use of plot conveys "more vividly than any naturalistic novel can, the social connection of individuals" (*EMF,* 48). And Forster's appreciation of the conditioning power of circumstance allows him perceptively to deal with the matter of class, and therefore enables him to make relevant for twentieth-century readers the great tradition of the novel of manners so dear to Trilling. In short, Forster's fiction manifests just the sort of social and political concerns that Trilling felt should be the special province of the novel. He says that as passionately as Forster is aware of the delicacies of the private life, "he is as passionate in his investigation of the complex relation between public and private and he has brought every subtle criterion of personality to bear upon the gross difficulties of politics" (*EMF,* 23).

Trilling's was the first major study of Forster's fiction and did much to introduce this novelist to American readers and establish his permanent place in the modern cannon. Forster said to Alfred Kazin in the early fifties, "Your countryman Trilling has made me famous!"[15] Trilling had not met Forster before he wrote the book, but just after it appeared, he reported to a friend that he had received a letter from the novelist saying that he liked the book: "it was as nice a letter as I would have expected from him."[16] And he wrote the book without knowledge of Forster's homosexuality, which may have been just as well. John Bayley thinks it "gains, if anything, from the omission."[17] William Barrett relates a story reported to him by Philip Rahv concerning Trilling's first meeting with Forster and his discovery of the novelist's sexual preferences. According to Rahv, Trilling was taken to a homosexual party in the East Village to meet the novelist and was aghast at his behavior.[18] Diana Trilling denies this story and provides convincing evidence that her husband's first meeting with Forster took place at a quiet and pleasant dinner at the Trillings' apartment in May 1949, on which occasion Forster charmingly helped with the dishes and fussed over the Trillings' ten-month-old son.[19] The two men became friends, but despite the friendship Trilling's enthusiasm for Forster's work waned over the years and, late in life, responding to a former student who had sent him some articles on Forster, he said, "Forster has come to mean a good deal less to me than he did the many years ago when I wrote my book."[20]

Chapter Three
Fiction

Critic as Artist/Artist as Critic

In notes for an autobiographical lecture prepared in 1971, Trilling says, "I am always surprised when I hear myself referred to as a critic. After some thirty years of having been called by that name, the role and the function it designates seem odd to me." By odd he does not mean alien, for over the years he had accepted the designation and been gratified by it. The oddness, he says, derives from his never having undertaken to be a critic. He had envisioned a career as a novelist. "To this intention, criticism, when eventually I began to practice it, was always secondary, an afterthought: in short, not a vocation but an avocation" (*LD,* 227). He mentions that "early, and in some sense abiding, intention" because it seems to him definitive of his tendencies as a critic. What he means is that his "conception of what is interesting and problematical in life, of what reality consists in and what makes for illusion, of what must be held to and what let go, was derived primarily from novelists and not from antecedent critics or from such philosophers as speculate systematically about the nature and function of literature." From novelists, he emphasizes, and not from poets. The novel, of all genres the least concerned with aesthetic shapeliness, is most concerned with substance and actuality and is therefore disinclined to claim it is self-sufficient and unconditioned. In taking its direction from the novel, says Trilling of his criticism, it has a tendency "to occupy itself not with aesthetic questions, except secondarily, but rather with moral questions, with the questions raised by the experience of culture and history." This tendency has a slightly antiliterary impulse, he admits, and is marked by an additional tendency "to be a little skeptical of literature, impatient with it, or at least with the claims of literature to be an autonomous, self-justifying activity" (*LD,* 227–28).

As a young man, Trilling was vitally stimulated by the great nineteenth-century novels, and he acknowledged several times their paramount role in his education. It was natural, therefore, that in contemplating a literary career he thought first of being a novelist, which, for him, meant applying imagination to social facts and moral ideas. "The novelist in his ideal character," he once remarked, "is the artist who is consumed by the desire to know how things really are, who has entered into an elaborate romance with actuality" (*GF,* 100). The novel for him was the definitive cultural document, "a kind of summary and paradigm of our cultural life" (*LI,* 250). This attitude is reflected both in his criticism and in his own novel. In his criticism he noted with alarm a decline of literary intelligence in the modern novel, a breakup of the synthesis of philosophy and precise social observation that he felt was the novel's very reason for being. In his novel he tried to answer the needs he, as critic, saw being unmet in the contemporary novel. In searching for a contemporary equivalent of the manners of social class which he found so fundamental in major novels of the past, he suggested by the example of *The Middle of the Journey* that it might be found in the manners of new groupings of diverse ideologies—communism, liberalism, capitalism, religious dogmatism. His fiction dramatizes his principal critical ideas. In fact, the best help for understanding and appreciating the stories written in the forties and *The Middle of the Journey* is *E. M. Forster* and some of the essays in *The Liberal Imagination.* Trilling's novel is so rich in ideas that one critic was prompted to say that it "reads at times as though it were first serialized in *PMLA,*" the scholarly journal of the Modern Language Association. This, he adds, is not meant as an entirely negative judgment. Intelligence characterizes the journal, and intelligence characterizes the novel.[1]

If Trilling had such a strong inclination toward prose fiction, why did he not write other novels and stories after 1947? This, he no doubt would have said, is a complex matter. He chooses to pass over it in the autobiographical lecture, suggesting that the opportunity for such an explanation might never present itself (*LD,* 227). Jacques Barzun suggests that the main reason Trilling wrote no more fiction than he did is that "teaching leaves too little energy and unbroken time for self-absorption, let alone for writing on a large scale," and Trilling "was cursed with a pedagogic conscience," a sense of duty to his students, both in the classroom and in conference. The critical essay was a more natural form of expression for him to engage in during the intervals between teaching, office hours, and committee meetings. Moreover, neither his own publisher nor any other encouraged him to write a second novel. In fact, says Barzun, his publisher, speaking to an English colleague who showed some interest in *The Middle of the Journey,* "shrugged it off as an unimportant excursion."[2]

Edward Joseph Shoben, Jr., a clinical psychologist and author of a book on the mind and character of Trilling, offers a more psychological explanation. He conjectures that when Trilling's novel was not as well received as he had hoped, he intensified his teaching and critical energies and restored his self-confidence by his success in those pursuits. Later, he began a second novel (he announced in a public interview in 1956 that he was at work on one) and struggled with it until 1965, when *Beyond Culture* appeared. That struggle, Shoben believes, accounts for the relative fallowness of that period. And because Trilling had achieved so much success as a critic, he was fearful to risk publishing another unsuccessful novel. The irony in this, as Shoben notes, is that while the 1947 edition of *The Middle of the Journey* sold approximately 5,000 copies, when a publisher nearly thirty years later requested to reissue it in paperback, it sold nearly 50,000 copies in the five years after Trilling's death.[3]

A more complete and authoritative answer to why Trilling published no more fiction will perhaps be available in the future. Diana Trilling intends to treat the question in a combined biography and autobiography she is now writing.[4]

Impediments and Departures

Two of the stories in *Of This Time, of That Place and Other Stories* first appeared in the *Menorah Journal* and are concerned with young Jews uncomfortable with their Jewishness. Written during Trilling's senior year at Columbia, "Impediments" appeared in 1925 as his first publication in a national magazine. "Notes on a Departure," published in 1929, was based on his year at the University of Wisconsin. The stories taken together reveal Trilling's changing attitude toward Jewishness during these years. The first criticizes a shallow and snobbish rejection of Jewishness and accommodation to the larger culture. The second portrays a young Jew wearied and bored with confronting his Jewishness and ready to put it behind him and start a new phase of life.

The narrator of "Impediments" is a student at a university, presumably in New York City, who is annoyed when the student sitting next to him, Hettner, forces an acquaintanceship by whispering ironic comments about the professor during the lecture and insisting on walking between classes with him. The narrator does not like this "scrubby little Jew with shrewd eyes and full, perfect lips that he twisted out of their crisply cut shape," who seems to have soul trouble that the narrator wants nothing to do with. He always tries to keep the conversation impersonal: "I felt always defensive against some attempt Hettner might make to break down the convenient barrier I was erecting against men who were too much of my own race and against men who were not of my own race and hated it." Hettner, he fears, might break into "the not-too-strong tower" he has built for himself. The two have quite different interests in education. The narrator wants facts—"quite lonely, quite cold, quite isolated facts"—that he can juggle and arrange for himself. Hettner, whose reading and knowledge are wider, is more intense and wants facts brought into relationships. As the acquaintanceship develops, the narrator does not mind affording Hettner fifteen minutes of his time a week: "it was amusing to ward off this puzzled soul as it groped faintly after me."

But then one evening Hettner shows up uninvited at his room, where he is writing a term paper on Browning, using the acceptable but painless "familiar formula." He senses that Hettner wants to talk about himself, about his soul. The narrator does not want to know about people's souls: "I like people's outsides, not their insides, and I was particularly reluctant to see this man's insides; they would be, probably, too much like mine." He is self-consciously literary and resents Hettner's shiny and worn blue serge suit that gives him "the look of a shop assistant." The talk moves from art (the narrator judges pictures by their signatures) to love to philosophy. "With a steady battering of talk he was trying to make a breach in my tower, to force for himself an opening through which he could reach in and snatch out my interest and sympathy, but I defended my citadel valiantly." While Hettner waxes grave and purposeful, the narrator remains cruelly detached and flippant, even when the conversation comes ultimately and inevitably to the subject of death. Exhausted "as though after actual physical effort," Hettner leaves in a rage, saying to the narrator, "What a miserable dog you are."

The narrator wins, but the victory is empty and merely demonstrates his superficiality and deficiency of feeling, his "underdeveloped heart." He is not capable of "the marriage of true minds" to which the title alludes (the lines from Shakespeare's sonnet are the epigraph to the story). His rejection of Jewishness is prompted by little more than a smug middle-class complaisance and a dilettantish literary bent. The story adumbrates Trilling's later preoccupation with the stubborn social facts of class and culture that became the central constituents of his concept of reality.

"Impediments" also demonstrates the flexibility and tolerance of Trilling's mind even as an undergraduate, for the narrator, so obviously satirized, displays in an exaggerated degree what must have been some of Trilling's own attitudes and characteristics. The story is particularly interesting in this respect in view of his later pronounced non-Jewish manner and his firmly explicit dissociation from Jewishness. "Impediments" must have resulted from an honest and penetrating self-evaluation during a period when he was genuinely perplexed by the tensions between his Jewish heritage and the larger culture.

Like "Impediments," "Notes on a Departure" is a contemplative story in which reflection and a little conversation take the place of plot and action. Once again the setting is a university and the particular scene the room of a young Jew. This time the university is in a small Midwestern town (a fictional version of Madison, Wisconsin), and the young Jew is an English teacher. The story opens as he is saying goodbye to McAllister, one of his students, a tall blond youth with a nursery stammer who, though only two years younger than the teacher, makes him feel "old, wise, and empty." Despite his appearance of youthful dullness, McAllister has been "a bouncer in a brothel-cabaret, a circus tumbler, a professional boxer and a stunt aviator." He has an unmendable broken rib endangering his heart. The town, like McAllister, "deceived by an appearance of simple dullness." Neither seems real to the teacher: "Some things were not real, even though one could talk of them confidently, touch them, live with and by them." Like McAllister, the town also makes him feel "old, wise, and empty." But whereas McAllister prompts shyness in him, the town generates fear. He has been here a year, and the town has intimidated him into "senility," "senescence." In order to prevent the town from including him "in a life into which he must not go," he has said, "I am a Jew." This phrase has acted as a charm or talisman to keep him free, but it has also increased his sense of age because he feels himself the embodiment of an "antique" race.

Like McAllister, the town bears "the sweet sign of eternal youth," and gyrates in "an unceasing vortex of youth." But despite their marks of youth, the teacher perceives in the town and McAllister "a spot of death," and this perception frees him of both. "He was free of the terrible senility into which they had pushed him. And he was free from the need for their kind of youth." Yet the freedom is not complete, for as he glances out his window and sees McAllister for a last time in his "green, irrelevant, unreal youth," he senses a residue of the same unreal youth in himself, a residue that may yet linger for a short while.

Soon after this, these peculiar thoughts are interrupted by a call from beneath his window. It is Enid, mounted upon a horse. He exchanges a few words with this beautiful young woman, reminding her that he is returning to New York tomorrow and will pick her up for the last time tonight. Then the thoughts continue, revolving this time around Enid. They have had a mild romantic relationship, but always with a dull barrier between them, "like a barrier of glass, neither could see it but both could feel it." He knew she was not what he wanted: "it was all an odd little religious pantomime that he had devised, and a diversion and dissipation of feeling and strength." Yet at one point she had touched him. In her company he had experienced momentarily a "sense of fitness, aptness, and justness" that had made him feel he was in a place that was his, "that had meaning for him, a nation, strangely, in whose center he was and he could feel it spreading on all sides of him, and, strangely again, America." The moment passed quickly and he could never recover it, but he treasured it as clear, true, and important.

The thought of returning to New York fills him with worry—about friends, competition, the justification of self, and the assertion of self—but he knows he must go and will not return to this town.

Finally, his thoughts turn to the question, "Jew?" He personifies it in two forms. At first he had made an angel of the question, "a pet angel" that he could wrestle with now and then so he could appear in company pale and drawn, and when people asked about his condition, he could say, "I have just come from wrestling with my angel of Jewish solitude. It is nothing, this pallor. A little faint I may be, but how strong is my soul." But later the question comes to him in the form of a red-haired, idiot-faced comedian, who pretends to choke him tremendously. "But he did not respond with the conventional gurglings and the exaggerated convulsions that were his part. He was passive and considerably bored." The murderous clown now sits down beside him. The teacher examines the comedian's face and finds it empty. He looks at the hands dangling between the comic knees, the hands that "had turned him for this place which, eventually but almost certainly, would have given him a very sweet and gracious contentment." Now they dangle without purpose. They have done their work and will not manipulate him again. He is free. But although those hands have stripped him for freedom, they have provided no weapon and pointed out no adversary. He searches the comedian's face again for something that would tell him "where to go, what to resist, what to make," but the face remains blank. He has been stripped, but given nothing. "From the angel he had got solitude. From the comedian he had got naked freedom, had got a clean-wiped slate, had got the readiness and ability to receive reality." Soon, he feels, he will "find his own weapon, his own adversary, his own thing to do, and this red-haired figure crouched by his side would have no part in his finding."

Out of this meditation on the angel and the comedian arises a new feeling, not of happiness or eagerness, but more of promise and determination. Although it is vague and indefinite, he likens it to an idea a writer has for a story. It may come in a simple sentence or a mere situation, but grows over many months until the writer finds it complete enough for the attempt to put it down on paper. And as he finally sits down, "he knows that his thus sitting down and beginning his first paragraph is the only thing he can do and the best moment of his life." Returning to New York will be the beginning of the paragraph for the teacher. The story ends on this qualifiedly hopeful note.

"Notes on a Departure" is puzzling because it was generated by Trilling's unique personal feelings about his experience in Madison and because, published in the *Menorah Journal,* it was directed toward a particular audience. The reader unaware of these conditioning circumstances may have difficulty understanding the self-examination that constitutes the story. Perhaps this is why the story has received little mention and even less explication.

Several items of biographical information seem necessary for a full appreciation of this story. Trilling was trained in and oriented toward the European traditions in literature and culture and was therefore suspicious of what appeared to him to be naive and less sophisticated elements in the American tradition. American culture had youth and innocence but lacked wisdom and cultivation. This bias was compounded by his being a New York City Jew with the cosmopolitan's usual condescending attitude toward rural America, an attitude tinctured with a certain element of fear. He went to Madison with these predispositions. Moreover, he went at a time when he was particularly unsettled about his Jewishness. These elements of snobbishness, apprehension, and self-division are essential constituents in the story. Trilling enjoyed some aspects of his experience in Madison, but America's heartland remained essentially alien and incomprehensible to him. It was an environment, however, that gave him a new perspective, and that year away from New York apparently enabled him to decide that cultivating Jewish awareness was not for him a fruitful option.

In light of this background information, the story can be interpreted as a description of several departures. The literal departure from the Midwest symbolizes a departure from a chronically innocent American culture. Like McAllister, that culture, despite its attractiveness and surprisingly adventuresome and sometimes sordid experience, remains unreal for the teacher, it remains perpetually youthful in a negative sense. The spot of death he perceives in it is its inability to mature and acquire complex and tragic wisdom. Another departure is from Jewishness. The question of Jewishness in its angelic and comic stages has reached a crisis point in this gentile environment and has put the teacher in a "state of readiness." These departures bring him to a threshold: the return to the worries and challenges of finding his place in New York, which for him represents reality.

Trilling has been criticized for being out of touch with the America beyond New York City. This story is fuel for such criticism. For someone from middle America, the teacher's reverse provincialism may seem silly or even grotesque. But taken on its own terms, and granting the sincerity if not the reasonableness of the feelings that generated it, the story is remarkably effective.

Teachers and Students

"Of This Time, of That Place," first appearing in *Partisan Review* in 1943, is Trilling's best-known, most admired, and most frequently anthologized story. Of all his fiction, it is most free of any instructive voice. *E. M. Forster,* published the same year, expresses admiration for Forster's insistence on "the double turn," looking behind an apparent truth to find an opposite kind of truth and then respecting the coexistence of the two. This characteristic of refusing to be conclusive, of knowing that no one aspect of a thing is the truth, Trilling linked with the "only connect" concept in Forster's *Howards End.* The two words are used as the novel's epigraph and appear within the story in this statement: "Only connect the prose and the passion. . . . Live in fragments no longer. Only connect, and the beast and the monk, robbed of the isolation that is life to either, will die."[5] This is what Trilling called moral realism, a recognition that man is neither beast nor angel, that good and evil, the rational and irrational, are inextricably alloyed. "Of

This Time, of That Place" manifests this sort of moral realism and attempts to connect "the prose and the passion." Trilling intended to hold in illuminating suspension the objective and subjective, precise and imprecise, rational and irrational, scientific and moral, sane and mad. The difficulty of maintaining the irresolution he advocates is evidenced by the tendency of the story's readers to favor one side of the polarities, even though Trilling, in his own commentary on the story, warns against this.

The story spans the course of a school year, beginning with the first day of classes in September. Joseph Howe, twenty-six, is beginning his second year of teaching at Dwight College. The author of two books of poetry and at work on a third, Howe has taken a degree at Harvard and gone into teaching because he had found the literary life, supported by a legacy, rather dull and wearisome. On this first day of school, two significant things happen. In class he meets an eccentric student named Ferdinand R. Tertan (Trilling pronounced the last name with the stress on the second syllable). After class he discovers himself to be the subject of an essay in the latest issue of *Life and Letters,* a magazine edited by a former member of the Dwight faculty and partly subsidized by one of the present faculty. The author of the article is the editor, Frederic Woolley, a defender of "the older values," obviously patterned after the New Humanists. His "Fifth Series of *Studies in Order and Value,*" and his former antihumanitarianism and concern "with the relation of literature to morality, religion, and the private and delicate pieties" clearly suggest Paul Elmer More and his eleven series of *Shelburne Essays;* but his turn to humanitarian politics is more reminiscent of Stuart P. Sherman. In the article, Howe is sharply criticized for the obscurity and "precious subjectivism" of his poetry, which fails to supply "what his society needs."

In the course of the academic year, Howe becomes involved with two contrasting students: the unstable but oddly brilliant Tertan and the duller but manipulative and practically successful Theodore Blackburn. The article in *Life and Letters* helps in developing the contrast between the two. The article arouses in Tertan a feeling of sympathy and kinship toward Howe, a kind of love. Blackburn, on the other hand, tries to use it to blackmail or intimidate Howe so that he will change his failing grade. Howe is forced, therefore, to confront the opposition of two fundamentally different personalities and sets of values. On the one hand, Tertan has the flickering fascination of the subjective and imaginative; he hungers for beauty and free spirit and intelligence unencumbered by convention and commonplace logic; but unfortunately he is deranged. On the other hand, Blackburn represents a dull practical intelligence, not very imaginative or perceptive, but possessing a shrewdness for getting on in the world—obtaining jobs, making money, using others.

In the course of the story, Howe realizes that Tertan is actually mad, not merely eccentric. He is reluctant to report this to the dean and see the unfortunate young man handled in the official way, but "without will or intention" he does just that, feeling both shame and freedom, a sense of treachery and escape. Meanwhile, again contrary to his inclination, he gives Blackburn the passing grade he needs for graduation. In the final scene, on graduation day, Howe, the dean, and Blackburn come together by chance as Howe is having his picture taken. Tertan comes by at that moment, and Howe thinks it must appear to him that the three are posing together. "Instruments of precision," Tertan repeats majestically three times and walks off.

In his own commentary on this story (*EL*, 781–84), Trilling explains that it had its origins in his feelings about a student on whom Tertan is based. Leslie Fiedler and others have identified that student as Allen Ginsberg, perhaps because Diana Trilling once mentioned the story in an article about Ginsberg.[6] But this is an error. The story was written before Trilling met Ginsberg.

According to Trilling, his first conception was "to present the sad irony of a passionate devotion to the intellectual life maintained by a person of deranged mind." He conceived Tertan as an impressive figure deserving something close to tragic treatment. Then it occurred to him to juxtapose this first student to another he had taught a few years earlier, one who provided the model for Blackburn. This juxtaposition would express the idea that "there are kinds of insanity that society does not accept and kinds of insanity that society does accept." Trilling assented to this idea but, with his penchant for subtlety and complexity, felt it an "aesthetic misfortune" that the theme of a story could be so easily formulated, and besides, this idea was not really what he wanted to express. Then he realized that having readers understand the juxtaposition of the students in this way could be an advantage: "For the story would seem to them to say one thing when actually it was saying another." He knew that readers would sympathize with Tertan and refuse to accept his insanity. And he was right, for when the story appeared he received many letters and phone calls from people disappointed that he had not made it adequately clear that Tertan was not actually insane. He took this as evidence of the story's power: "its ability to generate resistance to the certitude that Tertan is deranged." Furthermore, he thought the story challenges the reader "to reconcile two dissimilar modes of judgment with each other. One is the judgment of morality, the other of science." He acknowledges that the story seems to express the usual antagonistic view of literary humanism toward science, but warns that "this must not be accepted at its face value."

This warning has generally gone unheeded. The story is most often read in anthologies and consequently outside the context of Trilling's thought as a whole, which is so animated by an awareness of complexity and an instinct for irresolution. Furthermore, it is often taught and interpreted by literary humanists biased against scientific and business mentalities. The weakness, for example, of Diana L. George's generally useful essay is that it emphasizes the conflict of science and morality in too stark and unmodulated (to use one of Trilling's favorite words) a way: "To follow reason is to turn against feeling in the small but intense universe of the story. Science is the villain, totally correct but abominably immoral." She insists that Howe's knowledge, "an objective, scientific knowledge, is at continual odds with his moral perception of the situation."[7] These statements go too far. They accept Trilling's statement of his first conception as the central purpose of the completed story and ignore his indications that the story appears to be saying one thing when it means another and that the negative view of science is more apparent than real. Howe's knowledge of Tertan's madness is not purely objective or scientific. To be alarmed by an extravagant and incoherent expression of intelligence is a moral perception. And on the other hand, to ignore or excuse insanity in a sympathetic free spirit is not necessarily moral just because it is unscientific.

Trilling's attitude toward the oppositions in this story is radically ambivalent. Science, objectivity, reason, and authority can be dehumanizing in their strenuous, exclusive manifestations, but they must be given their due. A certain objectivity is necessary for obtaining the Arnoldian ideal of knowing the object as it really is. Instruments of precision are not to be despised, even though the mystery of human nature allows for only limited precision. It is useful to remember in this context that although Trilling's main character is a poet, and apparently a subjective if not obscure one, Trilling himself had no affinity for such poetry. For example, in a 1950 letter to Allen Ginsberg, he says, "Did I ever confess to you that my relation to modern verse is very largely academic and dutiful?—it seldom means as much to me as prose."[8] And in any final evaluation of his work, his values are much closer to those of Frederic Woolly than most readers of the story might suppose. Therefore, to view Tertan, as one interpreter of the story does, as "an inspired seer" with "an independence of mind and freedom of imagination that his teacher again forfeits as he rushes to join, lockstep, the procession of his peers" is to miss the complex ambivalence of the story.[9]

Once again Trilling's response to Forster is useful in understanding the fundamental vision underlying this story. He thought *Howards End* was Forster's masterpiece and particularly admired the way the novel treats the relationship between the person of literary and intellectual qualities and the nonintellectual, nonliterary person, the conventional person of business and practical affairs (*EMF,* 92–93). One represents the passion, the other the prose. The ideal is to connect the two. "Of This Time, of That Place" skillfully dramatizes the need, the complexity, and the painful difficulty of making that connection.

"The Lesson and the Secret," first published in *Harper's Bazaar* in 1945, is another story of a teacher and students. This time the students are nine wealthy women enrolled in a creative writing class, which meets in a beautiful, bright room of a city's new cultural center. Teacher and students surround a large glass-topped table. The broad windows overlook a lake. The animating tension in the story springs from the contrast of two kinds of success related to literature: the success of money and recognition and the success of truly engaging readers and evoking within them a new and vivid experience. This central tension is given resonance by the attractive classroom, the frequent references to wealth and social class, and the identification of the women with the past and the young teacher with the modern.

Before the teacher, Vincent Hammell, arrives, the women are discussing what they consider a lack of results: no one in the class has sold a story. The fact is that not all of them are even doing the class assignments. They come, apparently year after year, worshipful of "the potency that print conferred" and hoping to receive "the precious, the inconceivable secret" of obtaining that potency without creation. Hammell arrives, reads aloud one of the few manuscripts turned in, and entertains discussion. After a few superficial responses, the question the women are really concerned with surfaces: does the story have "a marketable value," is it "a commodity"? When one of the women suggests that she is interested in learning to write before learning to sell, a few of the others are swayed in that direction and the group becomes divided between those who believe the secret lies in learning how to sell and those who believe it lies in learning how to write. Hammell then reads a published story by a woman writer that tells of two young American girls visiting an Austrian village. The incident in the story is slight and undramatic, but the women of the class are obviously enthralled by it. The "quest for the precious secret" is abandoned and replaced by "a moment of brooding relaxation." One of the women captures the effect of the moment when she says, "Such a story makes one truly glad there is literature. We should be grateful." But the moment of contemplation soon passes, and one of the women asks, "Tell me, Mr. Hammell, does this writer sell well?"

The title is rich in suggestiveness because the story embodies several kinds of lessons and secrets: the class period as a lesson, the lesson about the nature of effective literature, the lesson Hammell and the reader learn about rich women who take writing courses; the secret of selling stories, the secret of writing stories, the secret of the motives for writing stories, the ultimate secret of why people respond to stories, and so on. But at the heart of this suggestiveness is what Trilling refers to in the final paragraphs of *E. M. Forster* as "the moral intelligence of art," which is an "intelligence of the relaxed will." Stories displaying this intelligence "drop deep into the mind of man, so deep that they are forgotten, so deep that they work without man's conscious will of them, and even against the conscious will" (*EMF,* 138–39). During their "entrancement," which had "something archaic and mythological" about it, the women in the class had such an experience. It came when the pressing will to find the secret relaxed into brooding contemplation. The story celebrates the mystery of moral intelligence in literature—the primary secret to which the title alludes—and examines the social factors, particularly the energized will, that inhibit receptivity to it.

"The Other Margaret"

"The Other Margaret" first appeared in *Partisan Review* in 1945, two years after the publication of *E. M. Forster.* It is a treatment of the moral realism that was the central focus of the Forster study. Like most of Trilling's writing in the forties, it is a critique of the liberal imagination. Its central theme is that wisdom, a bittersweet delight, deepened by the very discords that enter into its harmony, is aware and respectful of human complexity and is often painfully acquired.

Stephen Elwin, a publisher of scientific books living in New York City, leaves work early in order to pick up a reproduction of one of Rouault's paintings of kings. He has bought it because this king appears "human and tragic" and seems to possess a hard-earned authority. He meets a young soldier in the shop who, though polite, obviously has no appreciation for the picture. This encounter with youth causes Elwin, past forty, to remember a line from Hazlitt learned in high school: "No young man believes he shall ever die." This sentence comes to him from time to time like an explosion of light. Riding home on the bus, he observes an old bus conductor cruelly ignore a boy who inquires about catching the bus. The incident makes him angry and at the same time bewildered that he should be angry with "a poor ignorant man, a working man." And he realizes that he is angry with the boy as well. "The conductor and the boy were links in the great chain of the world's rage." Elwin leaves the bus puzzled and unhappy, contemplating the complexity of wisdom. "It seemed to him a great failure that his knowledge of death and his having reached the years of wisdom—they were the same thing—had not prevented him from feeling anger at an old man and a boy." Then he has the disturbing thought that he had felt anger "not in despite of wisdom but because of it."

By this point, the principal terms have been introduced into the story: youth, age, death, wisdom, and anger. Elwin then arrives home, where his thirteen-year-old daughter, Margaret, proudly fixes him his before-dinner drink. When shown the picture of the "calm, tragic king," she does not like it. "It said something to her that was not in her experience or that she did not want in her experience." Elwin senses in her response something "by which he could explain his anger at the old conductor and the boy and forgive himself for having had it." At this point, Lucy Elwin, the mother, enters the room, complaining about the other Margaret, the maid. This alarms the daughter, who is apparently attending a progressive school and has been taught by her liberal teacher never to criticize the underprivileged because they are not to blame. She is further upset when her mother tells of an incident on the bus similar to the one Elwin had experienced. In this instance, a conductor had made fun of a woman by pretending she was Jewish. Despite her liberal indoctrination, Margaret, in the course of the evening, is forced to confront the fact that the maid is indeed an unpleasant and malicious person. The realization is brought home forcefully when the maid deliberately smashes a green lamb Margaret had made as a surprise gift for her mother.

John V. Hagopian points out that this story of morals and manners is unusual in American fiction, in which the usual pattern is to treat such morally illuminating situations from the point of view of a child or adolescent. "The standard technique is intrinsically more dramatic and ironic, presenting bare action and dialogue, eschewing adult commentary, and putting the burden of meaning completely on the reader." Trilling's method is to present the conflict between youthful innocence and mature experience from the viewpoint of the latter. "This perspective makes it possible for him to comment explicitly on the moral issue in the story, and makes natural the meditative rather than the dramatic mode."[10] Trilling's preference for the meditative rather than the dramatic mode is apparent in all his fiction and reflects his inveterate concern with moral ideas.

The principal moral idea in this story has to do with human responsibility. Margaret defends the maid by placing the blame on society: "It's not her fault. She's not responsible." This prompts Elwin to recall with an "explosion of light" the sentence from Hazlitt, and he realizes that "in the aspect of his knowledge of death, all men were equal in their responsibility"—the two conductors, the boy, the maid, himself. "Exemption was not given by age or youth, or sex, or color, or condition of life." Responsibility, Elwin perceives, involves a "double truth": society may be responsible, but so is each individual. But what has death to do with this? Trilling was fond of Forster's statement, "Death destroys a man, but the idea of death saves him," and in *E. M. Forster* he says Forster's point is "that death and the value of the good life are related, that death is in league with love to support life: death, indeed, is what creates love" (31).

Elwin learns by observing his daughter learn. He realizes that "it was not the other Margaret but herself that his Margaret was grieving for, that in her foolish and passionate argument . . . she was defending herself from her own impending responsibility." The breaking of the green lamb, "a self-portrait," symbolizes Margaret's loss of innocence and confrontation with "the insupportable fact of her own moral life." The fact of moral life which Trilling had in mind is essentially the one emphasized in *E. M. Forster*: the world is good-and-evil, not good and evil. Liberalism resists this fact; moral realism accepts it.

The juxtaposition of the words "Margaret" and "grieving" in the first quotation of the preceding paragraph has prompted readers to recall Gerard Manley Hopkins's poem "Spring and Fall: To a Young Child," which begins with these lines: "Margaret, are you grieving / Over

Goldengrove unleaving?" The story and poem present an interesting comparison, and Trilling acknowledges in a letter to a curious reader that he had the poem consciously in mind when he wrote the story. He does not think that he began with a recollection of the poem or that his choosing the name Margaret was consciously dictated by it, but in composing the story the poem came to mind.[11]

Soon after the story appeared, James T. Farrell responded to it from a Marxist perspective, claiming that it is subtly tendentious: "We should realize that it is cleverly organized to present a reactionary moral view with insidious persuasiveness." The story is not what it seems, he goes on to say: "it is an expression of the general mood, the retreat from Marxism, the growing moral snobbery of the advanced and cultivated New York intellectual."[12] Farrell is correct about the story being tendentious; it is clearly a critique of what Trilling saw as the weaknesses of liberalism. And Farrell's response—finding the assertion of free-willed responsibility reactionary—simply confirms the existence of the tendencies Trilling was attacking. Farrell is mistaken, however, in identifying Trilling's view with that of the New York intellectual. Actually, the story offers a corrective to tendencies to which liberal intellectuals are chronically disposed. The critique is more expansively developed in *The Middle of the Journey.*

The Middle of the Journey

From its first conception, Trilling tells us, *The Middle of the Journey* was committed to history: "it was to draw out some of the moral and intellectual implications of the powerful attraction to Communism felt by a considerable part of the American intellectual class during the Thirties and Forties" (*MJ,* vii). For most American intellectuals of the time, the Communist movement of the thirties was a crucial experience. It was for them what World War I and expatriation had been for an earlier generation. Writing in 1966, Trilling says that "in any view of the American cultural situation, the importance of the radical movement of the Thirties cannot be overestimated. It may be said to have created the American intellectual class as we now know it in its great size and influence. It fixed the character of this class as being, through all mutations of opinion, predominantly of the Left" (*LD,* 15). Recent memoirs by two other New York intellectuals make the same point. Irving Howe insists that however much the New York intellectuals scorn the thirties or pretend to forget that era, it represented their time of fervor. "The radicalism of that decade gave them their distinctive style: a flair for polemic, a taste for the grand generalization, an impatience with what they regarded (often parochially) as parochial scholarship, an internationalist perspective, and a belief in the unity of intellectual work."[13] William Phillips thinks that "the thirties were the cradle of our entire epoch, and that we are still living out the unsolved problems—intellectual as well as political—first posed at that time. For what we think of as the contemporary mind had its origins in the profoundly traumatic shift of consciousness that took place in the thirties."[14] *The Middle of the Journey* was Trilling's attempt to explore the central ideological forces of this seminal period. Regardless of how it succeeds as art, the novel is a valuable document of an important historical moment, of a generation's conversion and disillusionment, resulting in a revised and subdued politics and a reconstituted aesthetics as well. The crisis in the late thirties affected art as well as politics, and this novel reflects the triumph of the relaxed will over the strenuous politicized will, of ideas in modulation over ideology, and of sensibility over propaganda.

Trilling was keenly interested in that radical decade, in its political temptations and its lessons of good intentions gone awry. He knew that his own intellectual development was strongly imprinted by it. It had taught hard lessons, and he could not look back to it without misgivings. In 1966, writing about being young in the thirties, he remarks that the period "left a sour taste in the mouths of many" and, despite its drama, ultimately "brought to the fore a peculiarly American desiccation of temperament" (*LD,* 4). He thought that the intellectual life of the thirties and the culture that grew out of it distorted and debilitated the emotional and moral content of experience, putting in its place a system of conventionalized responses. Diana Trilling has expressed similar misgivings: that time, "far from being the most moral decade of this century, the quickest and most irradiated with right feeling, was almost entirely built upon self-deception and the deception of others. . . . [In] consequence it left a legacy of debilitating ignorance."[15] Elsewhere, in a statement that illuminates the polemical purpose of Trilling's novel, she says the thirties were actually "a time of generally weak intellection—so many of us who put our faith in Marx and Lenin had read neither of them—but of very strong feeling. Everyone judged everyone else, it was a time of incessant cruel moral judgment; today's friend was tomorrow's enemy; whoever disagreed with oneself had sold out."[16]

So far as the novel had a polemical end, Trilling explains in the 1975 introduction, it was to expose "the clandestine negation of political life" which Stalinist communism fostered in American intellectuals. And this negation "was one aspect of an ever more imperious and bitter refusal to consent to the conditioned nature of human existence" (*MJ*, xxii). In other words, Stalinism and the kind of liberalism it spawned were forms of absolutism repellent to Trilling, whose moral realism demanded recognition, above all, of the conditioned nature of human life. As Norman Podhoretz explains, "Trilling was a central figure in the de-mystification of the Stalinist mentality, particularly as it affected cultural issues; and if you miss that element in his writing I think you miss what is central in his writing."[17]

Since death is the ultimate limiting factor, it is not surprising that the novel was initially conceived as what James called a *nouvelle*—a long short story with an explicit theme—about death. More specifically, says Trilling, it was to be "about what had happened to the way death is conceived by the enlightened consciousness of the modern age" (*MJ*, xii). Death remains important in the novel, which begins with an illness close to death and ends with a funeral. William Chace points out that "The novel turns, in its stately complexity, upon death. Death initiates, conditions, and gives character to, all of its main events. The people in the novel approach death in a wide variety of ways, and in their encounters with it invite understanding of their selves. Death, as it were, delineates and judges them. Thus it stands central to everything, subsuming politics as it subsumes all other phenomena."[18] But the treatment of death is not morbid, for Trilling had in mind Forster's dictum mentioned earlier: "Death destroys a man, but the idea of death saves him." Certainly in this novel the main character is saved by a new understanding of death.

John Laskell, thirty-three, an architect specializing in public housing, has been seriously ill with scarlet fever. As the novel opens, he is arriving from New York City in rural Connecticut to recuperate near his friends Arthur and Nancy Croom. Arthur, a professor of economics, has a summer home there. Laskell, a well-educated product of the middle class with an "air of maturity and responsibility" and the appearance of a man who takes life in "the sensible, normal ways" (6), is a liberal sympathetically disposed to communism. He does not agree with the Communist Party but wants it to exist because of its "clear relationship to the future" (62). It is the midthirties and such liberal fellow traveling is common among urban intellectuals. Actually,

Laskell is "not really a political person" and does not picture the world "as forces in struggle" (37). The Crooms, five and seven years younger than Laskell, are political persons and more seriously committed to Communist ideology. Nancy, as Laskell discovers later, has seriously considered joining the Communist party.

Accompanying Laskell on the train as far as Westport is Gifford Maxim, a mutual friend of the Crooms and Laskell. Maxim, a character based, as Trilling fully explains in the 1975 introduction, on Whittaker Chambers, has just broken with the Communist party. He had been deeply involved in secret activities and now fears for his life. He told Laskell about this just before they left for Connecticut and asked for help getting a job on a magazine so he could establish a public identity and thereby insure his safety. Laskell grants that favor.

Laskell's illness and brush with death have affected him profoundly. It "rested his mind and will" (29) and brought him a sense of "peace" and "strength" and "integrity" (26). It somehow involved "virtue" and "wisdom" (16) and a heightened awareness of being (48). He wants to tell the Crooms about it but hesitates because death does not fit into their scheme of things. There is no place for the tragic in their idealistic, progressive, and fundamentally naive political views. Death to them is "politically reactionary" (123).

He also hesitates to tell them about Maxim's defection from the Party and fear of being murdered. Laskell's illness and Maxim's revelation are linked together: both are the beginnings of Laskell's disaffection with the currently fashionable form of liberalism; both are jarring discords to the Crooms' fervent yet innocent leftist idealism.

Three other important characters are Duck and Emily Caldwell and their daughter Susan. Duck is the Crooms' irresponsible handyman, whom they excuse and idealize as a representative of the sacred proletariat. Nancy's admiration for Duck does not extend to his wife, however. Emily represents for Nancy an outmoded nonpolitical individualism that Nancy despises (87). For Nancy, Duck is "so *real*" and Emily is not (21).

The action of the novel is relatively limited. Laskell becomes friendly with Emily and her daughter Susan, and at the same time discovers that Duck is despicable. While fishing, Laskell encounters Emily bathing. Following a conversation in which she helps him understand his thoughts about death, they make love by the riverbank. He eventually tells the Crooms about his illness and about Maxim, and they react just as he had anticipated. Much to Nancy's displeasure, Maxim and Kermit

Simpson, the wealthy editor of the innocuous leftist magazine Maxim now works for, show up for a visit. The climax comes at a local bazaar and program they all attend. Susan, who, unknown to her father, has a heart ailment, recites a Blake poem, stumbling in an attempt to comply with Laskell's coaching. When she finishes, Duck scolds and strikes her for muffing the lines, her weak heart fails, and she dies. After her funeral, the group disperses.

Much more important than the action, of course, is the dialectic of ideas. Laskell's illness, scarlet fever, suggests both a "juvenile disease" (36) and the red associated with communism. It signifies a death that ushers in new birth, a transition stage from the childish to the childlike, from disillusionment to new wisdom. Although painful, the experience is also beautiful, like the rose at his bedside that he falls in love with. Abundant images of birth and childhood reinforce the pattern of Laskell's intellectual and political development established in the dialogue and the description of his inner awareness. As he emerges from delirium, the nurse tells him his name as "one often did with children" (42) and tells him his skin will peel and become "as soft and clean as a baby's" (45). And the child imagery is skillfully expanded and complicated in the novel by its application to Nancy and its literal embodiment in the child Susan. The motif of childhood functions simultaneously in the novel to signify, on the one hand, beginnings and the possibility for growth and learning and, on the other, arrested development, refusal of personal responsibility, and dangerous naïveté. His illness preceding the action that begins the novel is likened to the state of the unborn child in the womb (28); his moment of terror at the railway station while waiting for the Crooms to meet him is likened to "the moment when the foetus conceives of the womb no longer as the perfect place where desire and gratification are one" and desperately fears "the state of being unborn" (29). While rooming with the Folgers, neighbors of the Crooms, he often reflects on childhood and is playfully treated as a naughty boy by Mrs. Folger. This metaphorical childhood ends with the actual death of the child near the end of the novel, signifying the maturing of Laskell's intellectual and political development.

Ideas constitute the real substance of the novel—Laskell's inner perceptions and the concepts argued in the dialogue. Like Forster, Trilling took for granted the artificiality of fiction and conceived of the novel form as a structure of manipulated contrivances intended to establish a conscious end. And since he considered "the unabashed interest in ideas" to be a primary characteristic of the novel (*LI,* 243), he felt no compunction about devoting much of his novel to the description of serious thinking and conversation, and he felt no compulsion to be indirect about it. The book "coruscates with intelligence and dialectical sparkle," says Mark Shechner, "and it remains the most illuminating document we have of the recoil of the political imagination from dogma under the pressure of the chastened realism of the late thirties and the early forties—that fall into the quotidian that was the new era's particular form of disillusionment."[19]

Trilling's method, like Forster's, is to confront his characters with situations that unsettle their untested moral preconceptions, and the resulting tensions and readjustments become the essential matter of the novel. The novel vibrates with problems of morality that arise when political commitment becomes a mask for satisfying the needs of the personal will or when good people give the worst of themselves to ideological politics.

William Freedman perceptively delineates in the novel three closely related perennial problems: "the problem of human imperfection and its moral and political implications; the problem of free will and personal responsibility as opposed to determinism and social or metaphysical rather than private guilt; and the problem of how to deal with ugliness, evil, and mortality."[20] The three are integrally related to one another and to the process of Laskell's political maturation, which constitutes the novel's critique of liberalism.

Laskell confronts these problems primarily in the form of two opposing ideologies. One, represented by the Crooms, maintains that individual guilt and responsibility are nullified by the overriding forces of determinism. The other, represented by Maxim, maintains that all individuals are fully responsible and therefore equally guilty. Trilling's 1940 review of novels by Dos Passos and Waldo Frank titled "Determinist and Mystic" adumbrates this sort of opposition. Frank, says Trilling, "makes the familiar leap from the frying-pan of rationalistic determinism into the fire of mystic authoritarianism; it is a fact that will, I think, be emulated with increasing frequency in our time of political irrationalism, easy feeling, and undisciplined moral fervor."[21] The opposition is also reflected in Trilling's treatment, during the forties, of Dreiser's switch from determinism to mysticism or "pietistic religion" (*LI,* 19–20). Going beyond ideology, Laskell eventually arrives at a position of honest uncertainty: "An absolute freedom from responsibility—that much of a child none of us can be. An absolute responsibility—that much of a divine or metaphysical essence none of us is" (333). In response to this statement, Maxim admits that it aptly describes the hopeless extremes the Crooms and himself represent: "the child and the metaphysical essence." And he recognizes that Laskell seeks something between: "Call it the human being in maturity, at once responsible and conditioned" (335).

This mature position between is essentially Trilling's notion of what Keats meant by negative capability. In an essay on Keats, Trilling says, "Negative Capability, the faculty of not having to make up one's mind about everything, depends upon the sense of one's personal identity and is the sign of personal identity. Only the self that is certain of its existence, of its identity, can do without the armor of systematic certainties" (*OS,* 33). In another important essay, "The Meaning of a Literary Idea," he defends this faculty from "one tendency of modern feeling," meaning perhaps liberal activism, that considers it "an abdication of intellectual activity." He insists, to the contrary, that it is the very essence of intelligence to recognize irresolvable complexity (*LI,* 281). During his illness, Laskell had been "inexplicably interested in questions of being, in questions of his own existence" (163), and it is his new awareness of personal being that enables him to reject the "systematic certainties" of the Crooms and Maxim. A central point of the novel and of Trilling's writing in general is that the rationalism and idealism of liberal-leftist theory must ultimately take a back seat to questions of personal being, to the realities of actual existence in all its disconcerting complexity.

Liberalism that fastens obsessively on the future thereby diminishes its ability to understand and cope with the present. Concrete reality becomes distorted in an abstract vision of future possibilities. This idea, clearly stated in *E. M. Forster,* is a central motif in *The Middle of the Journey.* The Crooms and Maxim are oriented toward the future: Arthur toward "the near future," Maxim toward "the far future, the bloody, moral, apocalyptic future" (61). In the beginning, Laskell has a similar orientation; it is the grounds, in fact, for his friendship with Maxim and his admiration for the Crooms. But in a moment of insight during the process of his disenchantment with the Crooms' politics he has a sense that the future does not exist: "He did not mean that *he* had no future. He meant that the future and the present were one—that the present could no longer contrive and manufacture the future by throwing forward, in the form of expectation and hope, the desires of the present moment" (155). He understands that "maturity itself meant that the future and the present were brought together, that you lived your life *now* instead of preparing and committing yourself to some better day to come" (156).

The Crooms' fierce devotion to the future results in intolerance and absolutism. They display what Trilling saw as the endemic defects of the liberal mind: willfulness and rigidity; denial of moral complexity and evasion of personal responsibility; incompetence in the face of tragedy; deficiency of emotion; and failure of imagination. They and Maxim become angry with the change in Laskell: "It was the anger of the masked will at the appearance of an idea in modulation" (334). Actually, it is his perception of the will behind the mask that leads to his disenchantment with his friends, or, more precisely, "It was not their wills that wearied him but the necessity they shared to make their will appear harmless" (324). They are embodiments of what Trilling describes in his essay on *The Princess Casamassima* as "the modern will which masks itself in virtue, making itself appear harmless, the will that hates itself and finds its manifestations guilty and is able to exist only if it operates in the name of virtue, that despises the variety and modulations of the human story and longs for an absolute humanity, which is but another way of saying a nothingness" (*LI,* 87–88). The masked will concept is important for understanding not only this novel but also Trilling's criticism during the forties and fifties. His autobiographical lecture informs us that his task, as he saw it during those years, "was that of *unmasking.* Not merely of saying what lay behind the false representations, but of discovering and disclosing what was really being served in the personal existence by the attachment to Stalinist-colored liberal ideas" (*LD,* 240). He considers as one of the most significant moments of his intellectual life an encounter with a Russian émigré, wise and experienced in the realities of politics, who told him that "what motivated intellectuals was the desire for *power*" (*LD,* 241). This experience happened when he was in his twenties; it is the last thing he mentions in his unfinished autobiographical notes.

Criticism of the novel has tended to accept Chester E. Eisinger's dialectical scheme of interpretation: the Crooms are thesis, Maxim antithesis, and Laskell synthesis.[22] This scheme is essentially sound, but its oversimplification distorts the role of Maxim. He has been seen as pathological or evil or both. Neither Laskell nor Trilling had any use for Maxim's religious metaphysics, but Maxim represents a force of intelligence, conscience, and political knowledge that serve to expose the defects of the Crooms' liberalism. "Whenever Maxim speaks," says Irving Howe, "the book is brilliantly alive."[23] Maxim is uncannily perceptive, apprehending Laskell's thoughts and actions without being told. He is the asker of the hard, truth-revealing questions and consequently serves to guide Laskell to political maturity. He is a figure of moral conscience and voices on a number of occasions Trilling's own views. William M. Chace is correct in noting that when Trilling wrote his 1975 introduction to the novel, "It is Maxim/Chambers who returns with pressure and significance. Unbidden in the writing, and, almost thirty years later, forcing himself into memory, he stands for Trilling as 'a man of honor' whose 'magnanimous intention' cannot be doubted."[24]

The Middle of the Journey has frequently been criticized as being too exclusively a novel of ideas. William Freedman concedes that the treatment of ideas is admirable and dramatic, but insists that little else in the novel is dramatic—too little is left to our imaginations and emotions. Trilling, he says, is more interested in perception than action and "seems more interested in producing the effects we tend to associate with essays than those of a work of fiction."[25] Mark Shechner complains that "To throw the emphasis of dramatic action upon the collision of ideas in isolation, as Trilling does, is both to play up their historical importance *and* to exaggerate their political value."[26] John McCormick believes the novel's validity "is finally an intellectualized validity rather than an emotional one."[27] René Wellek says it is "finely written but too schematic and argumentative to be a good novel."[28] Even Irving Howe, who admires the novel, says that it at times reads "closer to a highly intelligent rumination about a fiction than a fiction itself."[29] Robert Warshow says the method of the novel permits Trilling "to deal with experience without compromising himself intellectually; it endears him to the reader for the qualities of his mind. . . . But he is removed from experience *as* experience; the problem of feeling—and thus the problem of art—is not faced." Furthermore, the method is ultimately founded on the assumption that "the most fruitful way of dealing with experience is to pass judgment on it—and this is not the assumption of a novelist."[30]

And the novel has offended certain liberal sensibilities. Trilling reversed the pattern of the proletarian hero of the thirties. His working-class people are not glamorized—quite the contrary. This has disturbed some readers who find his corrective to the pieties of the thirties excessive. Daniel Aaron, for example, sees "a certain bitterness, a certain coldness, a certain snobbishness, some might even say, in the values that are explicitly stated or implied in this novel."[31] Robert Boyer has described the novel as a kind of obscurantism, an elaborate pretext for the refusal of engagement. Though sympathetic toward Trilling, he is uncomfortable with what he views as the novel's quietism and accommodation, its preference for civility and decorum, its "wisdom of avoidance," its concessions and ironic retreats.[32] Readers inclined toward political activism are troubled by the way Laskell "earns points toward maturity and moral realism by declining to take a stand on anything but his own negative capability."[33] They view him as "but half a human being—mind without passion or the penchant for action."[34]

There is no definitive way to defend Trilling's novel against such charges. So much depends upon what a reader expects of a novel. Some readers are more engaged by themes and ideas than are others. They find the interaction of ideas dramatic, aesthetically satisfying, and not without emotional appeal. Others want action, intricate plotting, or emotional depth and complexity and will tolerate ideas, if at all, only when they are introduced with subtlety and indirection. It may be that those who insist that the "true" novelist does not deal explicitly with ideas or pass judgment on experience are unrealistically restricting a genre that encompasses many tastes and purposes. Trilling certainly thought so, and his criticism forcefully attacks the "prevailing notion that a novel which contains or deals with ideas is found to be pallid and abstract and intellectual." He argues for the place of ideas in the novel and for "the continuity of ideas and emotions" (*LI,* 257), insisting that "whenever we put two emotions into juxtaposition we have what we properly call an idea" (*LI,* 266). "Intellectual power and emotional power go together" (*LI,* 276). He claims for the novel "the right and the necessity to deal with ideas by means other than that of the 'objective correlative,' to deal with them as directly as it deals with people or terrain or social setting" (*LI,* 257). He remarks "how great has been the falling off in the energy of ideas that once animated fiction" and sees this as a decline or weakness in our general intellectual life (*LI,* 247). He was profoundly convinced that literature, "by its very nature, is involved with ideas" because "it deals with man in society, which is to say that it deals with formulations, valuations, and decisions, some of them implicit, others explicit" (*LI,* 265–66). "The aesthetic effect of intellectual cogency I am convinced, is not to be slighted" (*LI,* 273). Of course these convictions in no way establish the success of his own novel, but they provide illumination of and justification for his approach to writing fiction. And they suggest that part of Trilling's purpose in writing his novel was to demonstrate the continued viability of ideas for the modern American novel. As Marianne Gilbert Barnaby suggests, the novel is didactic, but it is a didacticism of craft, an attempt to show how future novels can be written.[35]

The art of *The Middle of the Journey* is certainly not without admirers. John Crowe Ransom offered this compliment in a letter to Trilling: "My feeling is that you have a *perfection* there—of tone and structure too—a finish and a consistency—which is very rare. Your book is first-rate, no doubt about that. . . . A book of old and standard virtues by a modern."[36] Morton Dauwen Zabel acknowledges that the novel is overtly dialectical, its language analytical, its structure polemical, its sequence of scenes nearly syllogistic, but claims that Trilling skillfully keeps the plotting "sharply dramatic."[37] Others have argued that although it is overtly a novel of ideas, it artfully manifests the emotional nature of political and intellectual attitudes. Some have recognized that in treating a particular political context the novel actually grapples with large and basic metaphysical questions. The influence of Henry James is obvious, and in capturing the nuances of unspoken communication, the subtle shades of human interaction, the novel often rivals James himself. David L. Kubal is impressed with the way Trilling used the structure of the epic to suggest thematic patterns, establish motifs, act as a metaphor, and furnish artistic discipline. The novel has twelve chapters, begins in medias res, and incorporates such themes as "the journey—here a psychological one—the recovery from near death, the love of a 'goddess,' physical combat, and self-knowledge." He suggests that the novel's title, taken from the first lines of Dante's *Inferno,*

> In the middle of the journey of our life
> I came to myself in a dark wood,
> Where the straight way was lost . . .

implies that Laskell's direction is through the netherworld.[38] And the skilful pattern of child imagery has already been mentioned. In short, the novel is rich in formal elements and craft as well as in ideas and deserves its place among the important American novels of its decade.

In an important respect, *The Middle of the Journey* was a turning point in Trilling's career. It was the last of his published fiction and also his last ambitious and specific treatment of political life. From this point on, explicitly political reflections are infrequent in his work. Although his writing after the novel continues to contain political implications, the political statements are fewer. Barzun suggests that "he purged all his political feeling of a polemical sort in that work."[39]

Chapter Four
The Middle Years

The Basic Concerns

The essays of the forties and fifties established Trilling's reputation as both a major literary critic and a subtly perceptive and influential analyst of American culture. Most of these essays are collected in *The Liberal Imagination* (1950), *The Opposing Self* (1955), *A Gathering of Fugitives* (1956), and *Speaking of Literature and Society* (collected and edited by Diana Trilling, 1980). *The Liberal Imagination,* the best-known and most influential of these books, propelled Trilling beyond criticism that merely explains the work of others to criticism that is literature in its own right, manifesting original and weighty ideas of its own. It displayed the possible force and breadth of literary criticism when its judgments derive from a comprehensive range of moral, social, and political concerns and from a distinctive view of reality. Beginning with *The Liberal Imagination,* the work of this most fruitful period of his career provides a penetrating critique of what he perceived as the errors and inadequacies of American thought and culture. The burden of that critique is the need for greater awareness of "variousness, possibility, complexity, and difficulty" (*LI,* xiii). Seeing liberalism as the dominant if not sole intellectual tradition of the time, he set about delineating the errors of oversimplification he perceived to be endemic to that tradition. He detected an inadequacy of perception in the liberal mind resulting from a myopic view of reality—an impaired vision of ambiguity and of certain troublesome facts about human nature. While avoiding partisan disputes agitating the surface of political and intellectual life, he focused on larger and less apparent social, intellectual, and cultural tendencies. His persistent inclination was to examine the imaginative consequences of our politics and the political consequences of our use or misuse of the imagination.

He found a ready and receptive audience among students, teachers, and writers disenchanted with the ideologies, slogans, and social realism of the thirties. He pointed a direction for liberalism leading away from the Soviet-influenced versions that many intellectuals of the forties and fifties found unsatisfactory. Moreover, his characteristic method of measuring modern literature and culture with that of the past, particularly that of the nineteenth century, appealed to an appetite for historical perspective that the future-oriented ideology of the thirties had starved. Although an academician, he was, according to Jacques Barzun, "the very negation of academic critic."[1] He was less the professional or technical critic than a sort of idealized general reader—intelligent, widely read, politically aware, concerned with large human issues. This sometimes irritated fellow critics, but the educated middle-class audience found it appealing. Some argue that Trilling's critique of liberalism was the working out of a personal crisis. Mark Shechner, for example, suggests that Trilling sought, through immersion in literature, to form a resilient self capable of confronting the perplexing demands of the age. Though this was a personal quest, "Trilling always treated it as the project of his generation through the neat rhetorical gambit of turning the experiencing 'I' into a 'we,' thus disguising the personal stakes involved and playing up the shared aspects of the crisis."[2]

The personal element in his analysis of literature as a manifestation of culture may account for the essential unity of his work. It is a unity of concern that is more real and significant than even he wanted to admit. His themes are relatively few and remain surprisingly constant from beginning to end of his career: literature as a criticism of life; the problematic but vital relationship between self and society; the perils of oversimplifying human nature and experience; the dangers of overweening intellect and will; and the complexity and pain of living the moral life. His detractors claim these were repeated with "little advance in sophistication and insight."[3] But his admirers perceive an evolving depth and scope in the repetition. In any case, Trilling asked essentially the same questions whatever his particular subject. Irving Howe, after noting that fiction writers keep telling the same story because it releases their fundamental sense of existence, adds that critics do the same: "Those who are truly engaged with the movements of their own minds also keep telling the same 'story,' returning to a single question or group of questions." This, he says, is particularly true of Trilling.[4]

Another source of unity in his writing was his primary literary interest, amounting to an allegiance, "in the tradition of humanistic thought and in the intellectual middle class which believes that it continues this tradition." What for him was so interesting about the intellectual middle class was "the dramatic contradiction of its living with the greatest possibility (call it illusion) of conscious choice, its believing itself the inheritor of the great humanist and rationalist tradition, and the badness and stupidity of its actions" (*SLS,* 120–21). This allegiance generated an enduring concern and anxiety about the welfare of the educated class. He considered himself the guardian of its interests and the critic of its ideas. Irving Howe says he consciously "tried to exert an influence upon the 'educated classes,' so as to shape opinion and mold tastes. Moving in the shaded area between literature and social morality, he kept steadily calling attention in his essays to 'our' cultural problems and 'our' premises of conduct. He had embarked on an oblique campaign to transform the dominant liberalism into something more quizzical and less combative than it had previously been."[5] Nathan A. Scott, Jr., describes Trilling's humanism as "anxious."[6] Indeed it was. A mind so committed to literature as knowledge and so obsessed with moral implications could scarcely be other than anxious in the face of modern literature. In a literary-cultural rather than a political sense, Trilling's idiom is an idiom of conservative anxiety. His essays manifest a quiet but persistent alarm at the apparent deterioration of the humanist tradition. R. W. B. Lewis, in a review of *The Liberal Imagination,* describes this anxiety as a "new Stoicism": "Finding it impossible to justify either assertion or denial, the humanist has frequently withdrawn to a doctrine of sustained tensions; and the courage, sometimes called the duty, to endure, in the midst of interminable and irresolvable polarities, tends to become the chief human virtue."[7] Irving Howe recalls that in his last meeting with Trilling he asked his friend if he was made "anxious" by the "recent high-powered methodologists in literary criticism." Trilling replied, "I always feel anxious."[8]

One of Trilling's anxieties was that the intellectual middle class was losing its understanding and appreciation of past cultures. Therefore, he stressed the importance of "the lively and informed awareness of another culture"—a culture distant in space or time which provides a basis for comparative measurement. This awareness trains both intellect and imagination (*SLS,* 356). Arnold used Greek culture. Trilling believed English literature and history could serve a similar purpose for Americans, providing scope and perspective. The culture selected is not as important as the act of getting beyond the perspectives and attitudes on one's present time and culture. In many of his essays he acts as a sort of translator, interpreting aspects of past culture (usually of the nineteenth century) and tactfully suggesting that they should not be undervalued, for they are related and relevant to the way we live now. He had recognized that Arnold "found it necessary to formulate a point of view which, while it affirmed the modern spirit with its positive goal and scientific method, would still allow him to defend the passing order" (*MA,* 206). He responded to a similar necessity, and one of his characteristic strategies was to bring to bear conceptions of self and society from the nineteenth century and earlier upon his consideration of modern literature and culture. He often used the nineteenth century as a prism that refracted the trends of his own age. Literature of the past century provided him perspective on present culture and furnished contrasts by which the literature of his time could be criticized.

Another source of the marked family resemblance among Trilling's numerous and diverse essays is the repetition of key terms and concepts. *Moral imagination, moral realism,* and *moral* as an adjective modifying any number of nouns occur frequently. If a concordance of his essays were done, undoubtedly *moral* would be a principal entry. Other recurring words are *culture, manners, politics, reality, will, negative capability, conditioned, complexity, liberal,* and *tragic.* Some of his readers find their use annoyingly predictable. Friends and critics alike find many of them elusive in exact meaning. The elusiveness combined with his courteous dialectical temperament enabled him to win a liberal audience for what, from a cultural standpoint, are really very conservative views.

What did he mean by *moral?* Joseph Frank labeled him "a critic turned moralist or a moralist turned critic."[9] These alternatives are misleading because they preclude the position to which Trilling firmly subscribed: criticism necessarily encompasses moral concerns. His concept of morality is thoroughly secular but not without transcendental nuance. In his book on Arnold, he quotes his mentor's statement that in us is a "central moral tendency," a "central clue in our moral being which unites us to the universal order," and links this with a statement by F. H. Bradley that moral judgments are immediate and intuitive rather than discursive (*MA,* 341). These notions seem similar to his own. In a 1949 letter to his friend Richard Chase, he mentions that Philip Rahv had questioned what he meant by *morality.* "What a damned word it is," says Trilling. "Maybe we have to invent another. But I profoundly believe that the people who make out to be ignorant of its meaning are off in a corner, however assertive they are, and that you and I know what we're talking about."[10] He never tried to define the word too specifically, partly because he enjoyed the latitude allowed by keeping it flexible and suggestive, and partly because he found it ultimately resistant to precise definition. For example, he describes a book's "moral reverberations" as "that strange and often beautiful sound we seem to hear generated in the air by a tale of suffering, a sound which is not always music, which does not always have a 'meaning,' but which yet entrances us, like the random notes of an Aeolian harp, or merely the sound of wind in the chimney" (*GF,* 37). This statement displays the transcendental side of his notion of morality. It is balanced by a rational side, which is best illustrated by a definition provided in his 1930 essay on "The Necessary Morals of Art":

> It seems to consist entirely of the admission that life is immediate to man, that life is his—his gift and therefore his duty—and that it merits and commands his best thought. It is not merely an affirmation of life, not merely a soft romantic yea-saying. It is something more difficult and more austere. A man takes the crude mass of his experience and upon it directs all the available force of his mind in the endeavor to extract meaning from it; by the intensity of his endeavor and by its success, the reality of his affirmation may be judged.[11]

This is a rational and secular concept of morality—nothing religious about it. It is strictly a matter of applied intelligence—man, unaided, making sense of his world. Both the transcendental and the rational sides of his moral vision come into play in his inveterate use of the term *moral.*

His assumption that criticism is essentially moral in nature inevitably led him to a preoccupation with culture and manners, which are the social manifestation of moral attitudes and values. He viewed culture as consisting less in great and good ideas and utterances than in social values and behavior. His fullest definition of the modern idea of culture is in *Sincerity and Authenticity:* "a unitary complex of interacting assumptions, modes of thought, habits, and styles, which are connected in secret as well as overt ways with the practical arrangements of a society and which, because they are not brought to consciousness, are unopposed in their influence over men's minds" (*SA,* 116). Culture was for him "the locus of meeting of literature with social actions and attitudes." Consequently, he felt that sooner or later "any critic of large mind will touch upon social matters" (*GF,* 112).

Culture is made up of manners, which he understood as "a culture's hum and buzz of implication." He meant "the whole evanescent context in which its explicit statements are made. It is that part of a culture which is made up of half-uttered or unutterable expressions of values." He had in mind small actions, customs of dress and decoration, tone, gesture, emphasis, vocabulary—"the things that for good or bad draw the people of a culture together and that separate them from the people of another culture" (*LI,* 194–95), all the outward signs of sensibility, judgment, and unconscious valuation. His use of the term *manners,* like the use of a number of his favorite terms, is complex and variable and has led to misunderstanding and complaint. He has frequently been criticized for restricting the novel to the novel of manners and viewing manners as the social conventions of a particular class. D. H. Hirsch, for example, complains that Trilling's use of *manners* is too vague to be useful and so broad that manners and their absence amount to the same thing. Meanwhile, what he really means is that the novel should deal with genteel manners "conceived from the vantage point of *haute culture.*"[12] Trilling acknowledged such criticism, mentioning that some had identified his use of the word with Amy Vanderbilt's book on etiquette. But he insists that his teacher in this matter was not Miss Vanderbilt but de Tocqueville, who makes manners "integral with culture" and says that they are "generally the product of the very basis of character." It is of manners as "the product of the very basis of character" that Trilling would speak (*GF,* 159). The great novelists knew, he says elsewhere, "that manners indicate the largest intentions of men's souls as well as the smallest and they are perpetually concerned to catch the meaning of every dim implicit hint" (*LI,* 199). Rather than trying to narrow the scope of reality with which the novel should deal, he actually aimed to restore the genre to what he regarded as its appropriate fullness and complexity, which includes the quotidian accumulation of actions, expressions, and signals that shape lives.

Trilling liked to use the word *politics* to denote what it was that he brought into relation with literature. His were literary, not political essays, he insisted, "but they assume the inevitable intimate, if not always obvious, connection between literature and politics." He meant by politics "the politics of culture, the organization of human life toward some end or other, toward the modification of sentiments, which is to say the quality of human life" (*LI,* iii). Because he believed our fate, for better or worse, is inevitably political, he wanted "to force into our definition of politics every human activity and every subtlety of every human activity. There are manifest dangers in doing this, but greater dangers in not doing it. Unless we insist that politics is imagination and mind, we will learn that imagination and mind are politics, and of a kind we will not like."[13] With this broad conception of politics in mind, he set out to convince the narrow political mind, the ideological mind, to enlarge its range of human awareness, and, at the same time, he sought to convince the literary mind to enlarge its social and historical awareness.

Nathan A. Scott, Jr., provides this explanation of Trilling's distinctive sense of *politics*: "his actual meaning is that, in a secular culture having the degree of complexity that ours has, the deep places of the spirit are, indeed, 'politicized,' in the sense that, there, a great legion of divergent ideas *compete* with one another for our assent and loyality."[14] When this statement was read to Diana Trilling, she said it was exactly right.[15] Trilling's essays, then, are political in the same way that much literature could be said to be political: as a response to the congeries of competing ideas, attitudes, and values of the time and place in which the writer finds himself. He once said that "every man of talent or genius is political who makes his heart a battleground for conflicting tendencies of culture" (*BC,* 107). Admitting that Trilling rarely wrote about specific political issues in the conventional sense of the term, Norman Podhoretz insists that "nevertheless his work is drenched in politics." He explains this by noting Trilling's "highly developed sense of context": almost everything he ever wrote "emerged from and was directed back into the surrounding atmosphere—a prevailing idea, a current attitude, a fashionable taste that needed correction or modification or qualification." And his sense of context was oriented toward contemporary American liberalism.[16]

Trilling's failure to treat specific political issues disturbs some liberal critics, who consider his eschewal of activism to be conservative or reactionary. Mark Shechner, noting that Trilling never wrote about such things as union strife, breadlines, and dust bowls, complains that he provided "only social sentiments and tastes which did not add up to an alternative liberalism, or, for that matter, an alternative conservatism."[17] William E. Cain warns that some of Trilling's views come "dangerously close to complete detachment and inaction in political life" and "should not be too promptly endorsed."[18] William M. Chace argues that "however much Trilling interested himself in the reality of political life, he wanted that life kept in its place. If it were, the conflicts between literary sensibility and social sensibility could always be resolved in favor of the former."[19] Liberal intellectuals have good reason to be disconcerted by Trilling's views. He devoted much of his career to criticizing their approach to politics. But they should realize that their demands for political partisanship or activism run directly against the grain of Trilling's mental temperament and moral vision.

To have acceded to such demands would have negated the mind undulant and diverse, the moral realism, the negative capability, that account in such large measure for his achievement.

The Function of Criticism

To understand precisely what Trilling meant by *morals, manners, culture, politics,* and other of his favorite terms is sometimes difficult, but any attempt at such understanding makes clear his conception of the function of criticism. Most central and consistent in his thinking was his faith in great literature as an agency of civilization, the best means for educating the individual to an awareness of variousness, complexity, and possibility, the surest aid toward the achievement of moral realism or the ability to formulate a wise criticism of life. Therefore, he is less interested in what literature is than in what it does, and for him "its function is ultimately the social and moral one of discovering and judging values" (*SLS,* 48). In its relation to life, literature is "polemical."[20] It is "tied to reality in a necessitarian way" and can do no other than "chase the reality of our condition."[21] The literary critic, therefore, must concern himself with more than form; he must treat the will, imagination, and moral vision to be detected within or behind it. For Trilling, criticism has to do with the quality of life wherever manifested, hence his focus on culture itself, on such apparently extraliterary matters as politics, psychology, education, and self-definition within the social context.

Over the course of his writing he was less interested in specific literary texts than in the effect that prevailing ideas, values, and ideologies have had upon the general culture. As he himself admitted, he tended "to see literary situations as cultural situations, and cultural situations as great elaborate fights about moral issues, and moral issues as having something to do with gratuitously chosen images of personal being, and images of personal being as having something to do with literary style" (*BC,* 12). As long as it resists the abstract and views culture "in its multifarious, tendentious, competitive details," the literary mind—more precisely the "historical-literary mind"—seemed to him "the best kind of critical mind we have, better than the theological, better than the philosophical, better than the scientific and the social scientific" (*GF,* 79).

Trilling approached culture through the avenue of literature, but despite his confidence in literature's civilizing influence, he frequently warned against expecting too much from it or taking it too seriously. In so complicated a structure of intellectual responsibilities as is involved in culture, literature's responsibilities must not be overestimated. If you ask too much from literature, he said, "you get far less than literature can give" (*SLS,* 114). He particularly disliked the tendency of leftist-liberal critics in the thirties to burden literature with "messianic responsibility," which it cannot discharge and which prevents it from accomplishing what it can do (*SLC,* 134). To require literature to be effective in an immediate practical sense, to ask it to do "the work of the will and earn its living by constructive activity" is a mistake (*SLS,* 150). It cannot save society or reform it. What it can do is provide a "contemplative experience" that supplies two things of considerable social value: an experience, justified in itself, of "unconditioned living," and "an awareness of the qualities of things." These two contributions "are, after survival, the great social concern" (*SLS,* 154–55).

Trilling admired breadth and diversity in criticism. This is reflected in his own concern with moral, social, political, biographical, and historical matters. "Any method which can bring enlightenment to literature is appropriate," he said. "Questions of philology, of biography, of social life, of literary tradition are all essential to the understanding of literary work" (*SLS,* 152). "The elements of art are not limited to the world of art"; they reach into life, and apparently extraneous knowledge such as historical context may heighten our appreciation of the work and our feelings about it (*LI,* 47). While acknowledging grounds for literary suspiciousness of the social sciences—misuse of language, jargon, use of unexamined assumptions while claiming objectivity, apparent denial of personal autonomy—he was nevertheless more open to sociology than were most other literary people. He thought such people are jealous that sociology seems to be taking over from literature the function of investigating and criticizing morals and manners. "Yet it is but fair to remark that sociology has pre-empted only what literature has voluntarily surrendered" (*GF,* 91–92).

It seems anomalous that Trilling's reputation was in fullest tide during the late forties to the early sixties, when the New Criticism was making its greatest impact. He clearly distrusted every version of formalism and used the word *aesthetic* with the limiting intention of denoting the inordinate attention to form as an end in itself and the futile pursuit of "purity" in literature. In a card to Jacques Barzun in 1961, he exclaims, "Nothing, *nothing* is more boring than *aesthetics*—long live history, long live biography, long live psychology! Only from these is art (as it is called) made." The card ends, "Yours in Herodotus, Thucydides, Vico, Michelet, Boswell, Freud."[22]

But although he disliked extreme forms of aestheticism, he did not lack sophisticated aesthetic standards of his own. And the remarkable perceptiveness of his occasional close formalistic readings manifests that he was not primarily a moral-cultural critic by default. René Wellek, providing for evidence a list of statements by Trilling, argues that he endorsed the main thrust of the New Criticism and consistently used the same standards as the New Criticism.[23] Wellek is essentially correct, but by omitting Trilling's pointed reservations about formalism, he perhaps overstates his case. Trilling provided a publisher's statement for Wellek and Warren's *Theory of Literature,* a product of formalistic assumptions, but he confided to a friend that he had "large reservations" about the book.[24] Robert Langbaum describes Trilling's relationship with the New Critics in this way: "Trilling's work was different from but not incongruent with that of the New Critics; they complemented each other." The principal link between them, he adds, was "the conservative drift of their criticism": the New Critics criticized liberalism from without, Trilling from within.[25] Trilling was sympathetic with the formalists' exhortation to return to the text, but thought the return must be followed by fresh departures into society, politics, history, and moral ideas if criticism is to take literature seriously as a criticism of life. The meticulous analysis of language is of great usefulness, he conceded, "but there are moments in literature which do not yield the secret of their power to any study of language, because the power does not depend on language but on moral imagination" (*OS,* 63–64). To the argument of critics who insisted that interest in biography or cultural context interferes with our direct response to the poem, he granted the merit of its intention, but then maintained that "the truth is that extrinsic information, whether we wish it or not, and whether the critics in their strictness like it or not, often does impinge upon our awareness of a particular poem and become an element in our relation to it which we cannot ignore" (*PEL,* 265–66). He admired what he recognized in the New Criticism as an awareness of complexity, manifoldness, and possibility. This aspect of it, he said, beneficially prompted him to press harder upon a literary work than his temperament naturally inclined him to do. But he was alarmed at the way the New Critical method had become institutionalized, because that militated against "the breadth and catholicity of reading which once was assumed to be the goal of the study of English literature" (*SLS,* 354–55).

The nature of Trilling's relationship to the New Criticism is reflected in his cordial association with John Crowe Ransom. As editor of *Kenyon Review,* Ransom invited Trilling to be a member of the editorial board, partly to add a New York voice to the magazine and partly to provide the balancing counterview of "ideological" criticism. After a few months, he apologized for the remark about the "ideological" approach, saying, "I think highly of your treatment of societal mission."[26] After three more years of association, he wrote Trilling, "Your interests and my interests don't always speak the same language but it is a great comfort to think they are pretty much the same interests."[27] And in another letter: "Certainly I feel continually more in accord with your own tastes and judgments."[28] That Trilling did editorial work for both *Kenyon Review* and *Partisan Review* indicates both his breadth and the nature of his achievement. While formalistic criticism was reaching a place of dominance in academic criticism and close analysis was perilously near to deteriorating into arid technical dexterity, he was insisting and demonstrating that the literary work is a nexus of ideas and values as well as symbolic structure. With tact and cogency he pursued issues usually reserved for sociology, psychology, or the history of ideas, thus providing an alternative or complement to the more hermetic New Criticism.

Style and Method

A large part of the reason Trilling could bridge the gap between groups as disparate as the New Critics and the New York intellectuals lies in his style and method. His supple, probing, unpolemical mind enabled his style, as Lewis Leary describes it, to circle "cautiously around the truth it seeks, tentatively, even hesitatingly, a step forward here, then sideways, or perhaps a movement backward, but ever circling closer and closer with quick eye and with a rhythm and grace of movement which certifies competence and insures success."[29] His dialectic admits the truth of one point while at the same time insisting that another also requires careful consideration, and then the two together must be joined with still other intervening assumptions. Stephen Donadio observes that "he was not inclined to knock down straw men: if he challenged a position he always did so at its strongest point, attacking what might be regarded as its fullest, most complete and intellectually defensible aspect. . . ."[30] Because of this, his judgments had more authority than those of critics who chose easy targets. His care and solicitude for all sides of every question produced a style of extreme tact and judiciousness. An early issue of *Partisan Review* contained a letter from Allen Tate commending Trilling's review of his novel *The Fathers*. The review, says Tate, shows "that it is possible for a critic to examine a work whose author holds fundamentally opposite views and yet convince that author, by moderation and intelligence, that the critic is disinterested."[31]

Trilling's characteristic method in an essay, as described by Irving Howe, was to begin "with a simulated hesitation but soon plant a hint that a surprise lay ahead, some revelation about the ways in which 'we'—'the educated class'—were misconstruing 'the cultural situation.' "[32] This is an accurate generalization, but more specifically, the "simulated hesitation" usually involved the introduction, in the context of a particular author or work, of an idea, attitude, or value from the past now ignored or undervalued by the "modern" view. The "surprise" comes when Trilling tactfully but firmly argues that the idea, attitude, or value is still vitally relevant. According to Robert Langbaum's description of the "typical plot" of a Trilling essay, Trilling begins with a positive position and then says all that can be said against it before returning to press for it. "The reader waits in suspense to see how he will make his way back to the original position, and is finally dazzled by the number of ideas, books, men and events that have been covered on the way." Langbaum suggests that, in an age of overspecialization, such essays are "clarifying and synthesizing because they bring together so many disparate subjects and contradictory directions in small compass."[33]

Trilling's discourse is marked by reticence, indirection, and disinclination for pronouncement, accusation, and invective. Neither shrill nor abrasive, the tone is that of rational discourse and modulated ideas. It derived from his notion of courtesy as a component of morality, an important binding element in society, and also from his belief "that objectivity in literary study and instruction begins with what might be called a programmatic prejudice in favor of the work or author being studied" (*LD*, 226–27). His style irritated some, for example, Delmore Schwartz, who found him often difficult to understand "because he is so sensitive to all points of view, so conscious of others and of opposition, so active and ingenious at formulating his own view in such a way that it does not seem to disturb but rather to accommodate and assimilate itself to other points of view."[34] But his choice of discourse was not simply a strategy or a manner; it reflected his sense of the subtle complexity of human nature and culture. Sometimes his habit of qualification has been mistaken for absence of commitment, but this is to ignore the firm purpose underlying his forbearing discourse. Dedication to cautious reasonableness and acknowledgment of ambiguity need not be inconsistent with moral purposiveness.

The Critique of Liberalism

No document states more forcefully Trilling's critical purpose during his middle years than does the preface to *The Liberal Imagination.* Trilling intended from the early forties to publish a collection of his essays, and this intention undoubtedly generated a certain unity in the major essays written during that decade and collected to form *The Liberal Imagination.* He mentions this unity in the preface as deriving "from an abiding interest in the ideas of what we loosely call liberalism, especially the relation of these ideas to literature." Two tentative titles suggest what he considered to be the focus of the essays. He asked Richard Chase's opinion of "Liberalism and Culture."[35] And among the 1949 letters to Jacques Barzun is a title page with "Art and Consequences" crossed out, apparently by Barzun, with this note: "L.T. = Impossible! Call it The Liberal Imagination."[36] Regardless of how it was arrived at, the title exemplifies the characteristic ambiguity of Trilling's primary terms. Is "the liberal imagination" meant positively or pejoratively? This is a matter of considerable disagreement. Liberals have tended to view the term as positive, but the fact is that liberalism takes a terrible beating in the book, its principal fault being, according to Trilling, a deficiency of imagination. The title can be construed as positive only in the sense of constituting an ideal by which the actual imagination of liberalism is measured and found deplorably wanting.

In the preface to *The Liberal Imagination,* Trilling laments that liberalism is the dominant if not sole intellectual tradition in the United States at the time, his point being that such dominance is not conducive to liberalism's real strength. What is needed and what he intends to supply is a salutary testing and questioning of current liberal ideas and assumptions. Viewing liberalism as "a large tendency rather than a concise body of doctrine," he suggests that some manifestations of this tendency will naturally be weaker than others, and "for liberalism to be aware of the weak and wrong expressions of itself would seem to be an advantage to the tendency as a whole." After summarizing some of the discrepancies between "the primal imagination of liberalism and its present particular manifestations," he announces his task as the recalling of liberalism "to its first essential imagination of variousness and possibility, which implies the awareness of complexity and difficulty." As he explained nearly twenty-five years later, he wrote during this period with "a polemical purpose and with reference to a particular political-cultural situation" (*LD,* 140).

Exactly what he meant by *liberalism* is problematic. It is one of those elusive protean terms used to mean so many things that their meaning is any particular context requires defining and delimiting. Even Diana Trilling is troubled by his use of *liberalism* and wishes he had defined it more completely and consistently.[37] Derek Stanford suggests that Trilling used the word in a wide sense, unrestricted by specifically political significance, and in writing of liberalism had in mind essentially the same set of assumptions as most rationalists have in speaking of rationalism: the belief in human perfectibility, a concentration on man's earthly existence, a bias in favor of utilitarian thought, and an optimistic faith in progress and rectification of wrong by reason.[38] To equate Trilling's notion of liberalism with rationalism in this way is instructive but not entirely accurate. In his view liberalism certainly is strongly rational, but it is also political, moral, and social, and should be informed by breadth of imagination.

William M. Chace argues that for Trilling's rhetorical purposes there were two forms of liberalism, a "good" and a "bad": "The former is inspired by Montaigne, the great hopes of the French Revolution, Mill, Arnold, and the nineteenth-century novel. This liberalism, '*ondoyant et divers,*' is friendly to aspirant and revolutionary individualism. 'Bad' liberalism issues from minds sunk into willfulness, progressive clichés, and imprisoning systems of political machination touted as benevolent, and from the suffocation of thought beneath the pressures of an obsessively militant concern with social circumstances or 'conditions.' " In short, says Chace, liberalism is for Trilling what his strategies make of it.[39]

Some of his liberal admirers insist that Trilling's target in *The Liberal Imagination* and related essays was Stalinism rather than liberalism, that his "hidden agenda" was a running argument with Stalinism, liberalism being a "code word" for Stalinism and all attempts to politicize literature in a gross, vulgar way.[40] And, indeed, Trilling mentions Stalinism specifically in his 1973 description of his purpose in *The Liberal Imagination* (*LD,* 140–41). But while he recognized Stalinism as the most glaring example of misguided liberalism, his critique of liberalism penetrates far beyond its extreme politicized manifestations. In his defense of T. S. Eliot's politics, he explains that Marxism alone is not responsible for liberalism's deficiencies; the central problem is "the total imagination of our time" which allows human quality to diminish before the exigencies of means (*SLS,* 165).

With regard to liberalism, as in so many other ways, Arnold was Trilling's mentor. Arnold had called himself "a liberal of the future." He wished to suggest by this phrase, says Trilling, "that he was in accord with all in the liberal ideal that was enlarging and liberating, and that he was yet not bound by the shibboleths of liberal thought" (*PMA,* 434). He was in accord with a "positive and creative" liberalism that conceives of life as "affirmative, interesting, complete, human" (*MA,* 387). In these terms, Trilling also could be viewed as a liberal of the future. As for the present, his stance toward the received opinion of liberalism was antagonistic to a degree his liberal friends have been loath to recognize.

To tabulate the charges Trilling leveled against liberalism during the forties and fifties is to recognize that with a friend like him, liberalism had no need of enemies. Many of those charges fall under the general category of a narrow and inordinate reliance on rationalism that loses sight of the complexity of human reality in its propensity for simplifying abstractions. In his critique of the liberal imagination during this period, Trilling frequently detected an inclination to deny the circumstantiality of human experience. He found that the liberal commitment to the rational reordering of society, to progress and perfectibility, often engendered or concealed an impatience with the stubborn particulars of man's personal and social life. And the impassioned concern with the future, so antipathetic to what he called his "thoroughly anti-Utopian mind" (*SLS,* 366), often produced contempt for the past and present and yearnings for deliverance from history. He thought that liberalism's hope for ultimate deliverance from human suffering and unhappiness in the external sphere of organized life was a rationalistic illusion, a form of abstraction. Happiness cannot be organized, and life's tragic contradictions cannot be rationally and technically controlled. Neither can the essential mystery of life be rationally resolved. The problem with the liberal intellectual, he said, is that "he was general and abstract where he should have been specific and concrete." This tendency "led him always away from the variousness and complexity of phenomena to an abstract totality of perception which issued in despair or disgust, to which he attached a very high degree of spiritual prestige" (*GF,* 79). And this disillusionment and disgust plaguing liberalism Trilling saw as itself part of a penchant for absolutes. He faulted liberal intellectuals for losing the centrist vision of man as neither beast nor angel and failing to recognize the full tension and polarity and modulation that belong to the essential reality of the human. Because it is enamored with the abstract and absolute, liberalism, Trilling indicated, can cope with neither man's immediate political problems nor the ultimate problem of evil. It is incapable of checking evil and injustice on the immediate sociopolitical level because it would like to operate against injustice in terms of perfect moral purity. And the ultimate problem of evil does not arise for it because it is always anticipating the perfect education or perfect social order that will make men good. In short, much of Trilling's critique of liberalism amounted to a defense of wisdom gained by full confrontation with life's tragic complexity against rational speculation with its inclination toward abstraction.

Trilling also detected in liberalism the "masked will" or, in other words, a tendency to disguise self-serving impulses and appetites for power behind a mask of "social consciousness." Of such social consciousness in the thirties, he said, " but how abstract and without fibre of resistance and contradiction it was, how much too apt it was for the drawing-room, how essentially it was a pity which wonderfully served the needs of the pitier" (*SLS,* 375). He claimed that Steinbeck's *The Grapes of Wrath* "cockers-up the self-righteousness of the liberal middle class: it is so easy to feel virtuous in our love for such *good* poor people! The social emotions can provide a safe escape from our own lives and from the pressures of self-criticism and generously feed our little aggressions and grandiosities" (*SLS,* 189). One source of sterility in liberalism, he insisted, was its frequent self-righteous confusion of a politics of opposition with a stance of purity.

Trilling's mind, ever on the alert for paradox, discerned in liberalism a number of disturbing paradoxes. He pointed out, for example, that although liberalism is concerned above all else with emotions, to establish their importance it "tends to deny them their full possibility." He meant that liberalism values emotions and variousness and possibility in the abstract, but the conscious and unconscious life of liberalism are not always in accord (*LI,* x–xi). A second and related paradox is that liberalism, "in the very interest of affirming its confidence in the power of the mind," inclines "to constrict and make mechanical its conception of the nature of mind" by denying the emotions and imagination (*LI,* xi). Another paradox is that liberalism's notion of "reality" apparently prefers "unpleasant bedrock facts" (witness the vogue of social realism in the thirties), yet what it says about that reality tends toward the abstract and indicates a desire to escape from conditioned actualities of ordinary social experience (*LI,* 303.) Still another paradox is that while liberalism envisions freedom and moral possibility, its programs unexpectedly work to diminish them and are unconsciously repressive: "It is a tragic irony that the diminution of the moral possibility, with all that the moral possibility implies of free will and individual value, should spring, as it does, from the notion of the perfectibility of man" (*SLS,* 166–67). Finally, there is the tragic paradox of the dangers that lie in liberalism's most generous wishes: "Some paradox of our nature leads us, when once we have made our fellow men the objects of our enlightened interest, to go on to make them the objects of our pity, then of our wisdom, ultimately of our coercion" (*LI,* 208).

In view of Trilling's extended and rigorous critique of liberalism, questions naturally arise concerning his loyalty to liberalism. The fact is that his thought is characterized by some strong and fundamental conservative qualities, which have largely been ignored because most of those who have analyzed or commented on his criticism have been liberal intellectuals. This group has tended to see him as a model liberal with grace enough to acknowledge liberalism's imperfections. A notable exception to this pattern is Joseph Frank's 1956 essay "Lionel Trilling and the Conservative Imagination," which had an effect much like the boy's statement that the emperor was wearing no clothes. Frank explicitly aligns Trilling with "Babbitt, More and the American Humanists," calling him "one of the least belligerent and most persuasive spokesmen of the conservative imagination."[41] He sees Trilling's moderation and insistence on moral realism as a kind of restatement of Babbitt and More's "inner check." He meant this derogatorily, of course, and considered his discovery rather shocking.

Trilling himself did not want to be considered a conservative during the forties and fifties. He thought of himself as a liberal criticizing liberalism in order to preserve the liberal principle. That he often was, in fact, conservative in argument and sensibility was an imputation he strongly resisted. William Phillips recalls that one of the few times he saw Trilling lose his calm was when he suggested that Trilling was being read as a conservative thinker and he ought to be more aware of the inflection of his writing. Trilling said angrily that he did not care what people thought.[42] This may have been a case of protesting too much, for later in his career, as William M. Chace argues, the imputation of conservatism "would be received more warmly, would be seen not as a 'charge' but as a kind of praise."[43] Trilling obviously adhered to the Enlightenment tradition and favored the values of tolerance and public freedoms, but, recalls Irving Howe, "if one meant by 'liberal'—as in post–New Deal America one had also to mean—a militant politics in behalf of both social reform and a measure of egalitarianism, then the effect of Trilling's essays was to dissuade people from that brand of liberalism."[44] As Trilling used the term, Howe remarks elsewhere, it included "a kind of conservatism" and "was more a moral imaginative stance than a concrete politics." His sense of liberalism was at times "almost the equivalent of moral imagination, of richness, diversity, complexity, openness of mind."[45]

Trilling detested being labeled or characterized because he felt it limited him and created predispositions in his readers. He desired latitude and a reputation for tolerant objectivity. This sometimes kept even his friends guessing. William Phillips thought he often appeared conservative just as a way of distinguishing himself from pro-Communist liberals.[46] Delmore Schwartz, on the other hand, accused him of using *Partisan Review* to "protect his left flank." By appearing in a left-wing magazine he could hide how conservative his real message was.[47] And it is true that his liberal reputation enabled him to get away with a good deal. As William Van O'Connor remarked in 1950, Trilling made statements in *The Liberal Imagination* that, "uttered by a critic not equally free of suspicion, would have brought symbolic exile to Siberia, Rome, the deep South, or the offices of the *Herald Tribune*."[48]

The vitalizing tensions of Trilling's intellectual development derive ultimately from the fact that he was a liberal—the product of a liberal environment to which he was strongly attached—who discovered that an intelligent case could be made for the conservative side, and this discovery was an intellectual awakening. The burden of his subsequent intellectual career was an attempt to bring his liberal and conservative tendencies of mind into logical relation, a task that naturally involved an exploration of the relation of these opposing impulses within the culture where he had encountered them. This attempt accounts for the impression of ambivalence and dialectical brilliance that characterize much of his writing. And it took him to the edges of liberalism. As William M. Chace explains, "The ground beneath him was again and again found to be either weak or worthy of being forfeited. So, bit by bit, he gave ground over the years until what was left to him was only sentiments residual within the liberal tradition—a sense of expanded mental and moral faculties, a preference for curiosity, a vague encouragement toward the liberation of self from whatever might constrain self."[49] Meanwhile, he was continuously coming to value certain conservative sentiments—not conservative doctrines, but temperamental dispositions; and not a conservative politics, for his direction was essentially apolitical in the usual narrow sense of "politics."

Viewed from the eighties, the conservative thrust of Trilling's criticism is strikingly manifest. Considering the New Humanism of the twenties and the poststructuralism of the eighties as poles of a continuum, one must locate Trilling very near the former. When the New Humanism is objectively viewed and Trilling's liberalism is accurately discerned, numerous parallels emerge within the writings of Trilling, Irving Babbitt, and Paul Elmer More. The similarities have been mentioned in asides and footnotes but not adequately acknowledged and explored.[50] This is not to suggest a direct influence, although Trilling quotes both Babbitt and More in *Matthew Arnold* (104, 343). The similarities are mostly due to the common influence of Arnold and the classical humanist tradition that produced him. Trilling, however, was influenced by the European rather than the American Arnoldian tradition, and, as a New York Jewish intellectual, his proclivity for moral concerns was largely shaped by the anguished moral struggling of nineteenth-century European intellectuals. Babbitt and More, on the other hand, were both Midwesterners and derived their moral concerns largely from American Protestantism. The tradition Arnold, and in turn the New Humanists, represented and furthered included, according to Paul Elmer More, Cicero, Erasmus, Boileau, Shaftesbury, and Sainte-Beuve. It renders literature "more consciously a criticism of life," and its representatives are "discriminators between the false and the true, the deformed and the normal, preachers of harmony and proportion and order, prophets of the religion of taste." They use the past for models and are ever "checking the enthusiasm of the living by the authority of the dead." They are "by intellect hesitators, but at heart very much in earnest." They stand with the great conservative forces of human nature, "having their fame certified by the things that endure amid the betrayals of time and fashion."[51] Trilling, despite his rational, secular, liberal cast of mind, is not at all alien to this conservative tradition.

Freud and Culture

Writing to Jacques Barzun in 1938, Trilling said, "I feel that the man who undertakes a sympathetic but critical consideration of psychoanalysis will be doing one of the real jobs of the generation."[52] This job became for him an enduring and engrossing preoccupation. Beginning with an invitation from John Crowe Ransom in 1939 to write for *Kenyon Review* an article on the use of Freudian concepts by artists, critics, and aestheticians, he became one of the first critics of standing to write at length and with authority of the relationship between psychoanalysis and literature. His conclusions were conservative and judicious, and his suggestions for new applications of Freud's thought to the literary analysis of culture were brilliant. Freud became a decisive influence upon his thought, and the dominant themes in his critique of liberal culture during the forties and fifties grew in tandem with his interest in psychoanalysis, Freud providing much of the groundwork for his criticism of liberalism. Two of his major essays on Freud, "Freud and Literature" and "Art and Neurosis," appear in *The Liberal Imagination.* A third, "Freud: Within and Beyond Culture," appears in *Beyond Culture.* And a number of shorter essays on Freud and frequent references to him appear throughout Trilling's writing. His interest in Freud frequently centered on the nexus of overt and hidden, public and private, conscious and unconscious. Just as Freud examined trivial actions of the individual as clues to unconscious desires and attitudes, Trilling examined manners and morals in society as clues to inconspicuous but potent cultural tendencies.

Freud was second only to Arnold as an influence upon Trilling, and it must be remembered that a secular mind such as Trilling's, lacking the resource of supernatural authority, is greatly dependent upon the example and authority of great and wise men. Consequently, the influence exerted upon him by Arnold and Freud goes beyond the usual notions of influence. They were for him exemplary and representative men, models of intellectual virtue, clarifiers and fulfillers of the central thrust of Western thought. Because they fused the ideals of the Enlightenment with a profound tragic sense of human complexity, they treated the problems central to modern life. For Trilling, they complemented each other: Arnold speaks to us of the value of high culture, Freud of the discontents of civilization. Between them they express the range of social possibility, and between them Trilling sustains his own dialectic. Trilling shared Arnold's recognition of the importance of balancing intellect with emotion and spirit, but, being secularly oriented, he looked to science rather than to religion for information about man's nature, and his main frame of reference became Freudian psychology. He shared Arnold's quest for a society of intelligence, tolerance, and flexibility, but could not look for help, as Arnold did, from the state or Christianity, so he turned to Freudian psychology as a buttress for his cherished values. R. P. Blackmur suggests that Trilling "corrects" his two masters: "Because of Freud, the contingency of incentive and dread is clearer than in Arnold; because of Arnold, the intellectuality and sanity of art are clearer than in Freud."[53]

It would be difficult to overestimate the effect of Freud upon Trilling's thought. "Freud is one of the very greatest figures of our epoch," he said. "His effect upon contemporary thought and assumption is incalculable" (*SLS,* 270–71), "he ultimately did more for our understanding of art than any other writer since Aristotle" (*LI,* 153), and he was "one of the very greatest of humanistic minds" (*BC,* 79). William Barrett suggests that if Trilling could be called doctrinaire about anything, it is his adherence to Freudianism: "Freud is the one fixed pillar of conviction to which he personally held," and when he invokes Freud's name, "it is nearly always bathed in something of a numinous glow."[54] Trilling was drawn to Freud's character as much as to his thought, and Freud's moral style interested him as much as his scientific ideas. In Trilling's view, Freud not only identified the central difficulties in social existence but provided a model for courageously confronting them, for managing tensions and achieving selfhood. He found Freud's unillusioned fortitude and probing curiosity, both grounded in secularism and rationalism, congenial and worthy of emulation. Steven Marcus, who with Trilling edited an abridgment of Ernest Jones's three-volume *The Life and Work of Sigmund Freud,* explains that "the figure of Freud was for him something very close to a moral ideal, or to an ideal of personal character and conduct. Freud's fierceness, boldness, honesty and independence, his sense of tragedy and stoical resistance all served or figured as models for him, models that he reaffirmed in his own person and tried to fulfill in his own existence."[55] Throughout his career, Trilling regarded Freud as the guarantor of his highest values, which were centered in the Western tradition of classic tragic realism.

Trilling possessed a reasonably comprehensive knowledge of Freudian psychology, enough to be the first layman invited to lecture on Freud to the New York Psychoanalytical Society, but his interest was selective. In regard to Freud as with liberalism, he took issue with people on his own side while moving in a conservative direction. He was doubtful about the analytical ability of psychoanalysis to fathom literature and consequently was rather critical of Freud's early analytical works. He was more interested in the later works that treated social, cultural, and metaphysical questions. As he acknowledges in his autobiographical lecture, Freud's "decisive" influence upon him did not take the form of "doctrinal authority." Instead, it exerted itself as a forceful awareness of "the actuality and intimacy of history, of society, of culture" and a felt necessity of "discovering the causative principles of these entities" (*LD,* 237). He considered *Beyond the Pleasure Principle* and *Civilization and Its Discontents* to be Freud's most important and relevant works, viewing the latter as an indispensible milestone in Western cultural history for its conclusion that discontent is inherent in the condition of man in culture. The ideas of this little book dominated and preoccupied him throughout his career, and it became a standard offering in his modern literature courses. Mark Schechner insists that "much of what passes for Freudian thought in Trilling's writing is really applied *Civilization and Its Discontents.*"[56]

It was not Freud as clinician or as discriminator among neuroses that interested him, but rather Freud as philosopher of culture, as tragic humanist, as prophetic student of humanity's great aspirations and great limitations. Thus, in the tragic perspective of Freudian thought, he sensed a kind of stern and lofty poetry and suggests that Freud's last book, *An Outline of Psychoanalysis,* can provide "a great intellectual, moral, and even aesthetic experience" (*GF,* 61). "The pleasure I have in responding to Freud," he says in another essay with reference to the same book, "I find very difficult to distinguish from the pleasure which is involved in responding to a satisfactory work of art" (*LI,* 273–74).

It is with this tragic Freud, the Freud of *Civilization and Its Discontents,* unsympathetic to all notions of humanitarian optimism, that he confronted American liberals. *Civilization and Its Discontents* substantiated for him the need of moral realism and contributed to the conservative element in his thought. He complained that the book has not been adequately appreciated and consequently Freud's ideas have been misunderstood and developed in unsatisfactory ways. We have not understood that they contain "the elements of a most complex moral system" (*GF,* 82). In a letter to Mark Van Doren he decried "shabby popularizations" of Freudian ideas, most of which were actually "antagonistic revisions and softenings of his theory."[57] He saw Karen Horney's adaptation of Freud as symptomatic "of one of the great inadequacies of liberal thought, the need for optimism." Insisting on the dark, tragic elements in Freud, he extols Freud's courage in daring "to present man with the terrible truth of his own nature" and to suggest "the savage difficulties of life" (*SLS*, 184–85). He liked

Norman O. Brown's *Life against Death* at least for this: "It represents psychoanalysis not as it is blandly conceived by the progressive wing of the middle class, but in all its bitter complexity, in all its uncompromising tragic force" (*SLS*, 362–63).

Trilling's Freud is selective and idealized. The man overshadows the method, and some claim his admiration for the man as moralist caused him to misread the implications of what the positivist psychologist actually taught. William Barrett asserts that Trilling chose not to see the negative and reductive side of Freud, and that when Trilling says he responds to Freud in much the same way he responds to a satisfactory work of art, we must realize he is reading another Freud, "a poem that he himself has created."[58] Obviously, Trilling was never much interested in some of Freud's technical or clinical formulations, and his uses of Freud include nearly nothing of the early empirically scientific work. He manifests little interest in Freud's ideas concerning such things as infantile sexuality, guilt, dreams, the psychology of jokes, repression, and the specific dynamics of the unconscious. Steven Marcus says Trilling was interested in Freud because Trilling's interest in literature was partly moral, psychological, and cultural and because Freud was a great literary figure. But "whenever Freud made some reductive or positivist kind of statement Trilling would tend either to disregard it or point to something else."[59]

If so much of Freud is missing in Trilling's conception of Freudianism, what remains? Mark Shechner, in a very informative treatment of Trilling and psychoanalysis, explains that Trilling retained Freud's structural or dialectical model of the mind with its intrapsychic dynamism of ego, id, and superego, and he adopted the cultural dialectic, "the struggle of the ego to claim a niche for itself between instinct and culture," so important in *Civilization and Its Discontents.* But most of the Freudianism that informs Trilling's writing results from his admiration for Freud's character: "his commitment to secular rationalism and his stands against the delusions of mythic and religious thinking, his wary and grudging approval of culture, his refusal to allow disappointment, resistance, and pain to weaken his convictions or interfere with his work, and his very definition of mental health as the capacity for love and work."[60]

Shechner notes, as others have done, the remarkable discrepancy between Trilling's zeal for Freud and his actual uses of him. For all his stress on Freud's achievement, Trilling's own attitude toward psychoanalysis was reticent and ambivalent, and he sometimes scrupulously avoided deploying its method with full rigor even in instances that seemed to warrant it. "Nowhere in his work," says Shechner, "do we find an instance of relentless psychoanalytic pursuit of latent meanings or a reaching after those distressing conclusions about infantile needs and irrational drives that are the special province of psychoanalysis as an interpretive system."[61] Trilling, of course, was leery of systems, partly as a result of his disillusionment with Marxist criticism in the twenties and thirties, and so he came to Freud with scruples and habits of skepticism about systems. Louis Fraiberg also notes in Trilling's approach to psychoanalysis "a hesitation, a gingerly handling and a series of hedgings of denials."[62] Trilling had three large reservations about the ability of psychoanalysis to enlighten us about art and culture. He was troubled by its reluctance "to deal with artistic success as being as much implicated in neurosis as is artistic failure"; its restriction of its purview "to the individual artist, without reference to the culture in which he performs"; and its lack of awareness of its own limits. In elaborating this last point, he alleges that psychoanalytic criticism is "wholly at a loss when it touches upon the question of how the nexus between personality and creative power is made," and that it "virtually never addresses itself to questions of language, of style, or dramatic form" (*SLS,* 397, 317).

The essential reason Trilling did not practice psychoanalytic criticism in any overt or systematic way is that he temperamentally distrusted the diagnostic reduction of complex feelings and perceptions, and he was also temperamentally disposed to examine literature as an agent of moral and psychological health. As Shechner perceptively observes, "As a partisan of literature he was distressed by the psychoanalytic practice of analyzing downward in pursuit of reality among the infantile, the somatic, the irrational, and the unconscious levels of being. . . . His inclination was to analyze upward toward the artist's moral posture, even toward the morality of art itself."[63]

Literature and Ideas

Trilling could respond aesthetically to Freud because of his notion that ideas are integral to the aesthetic experience taken in any meaningful sense. "The aesthetic effect of intellectual cogency, I am convinced, is not to be slighted" (*LI,* 273). This statement comes from "The Meaning of a Literary Idea," in which he argues that literature, "by its very nature, is involved with ideas" because "it deals with man in society, which is to say that it deals with formulations, valuations, and decisions, some of them implicit, others explicit." Whenever two emotions are juxtaposed, "we have what we properly call an idea" (*LI,* 265–66). Because he thought intellectual and emotional power are implicated in each other, forming a continuity of ideas and emotions, he found that certain kinds of ideas are not hostile to the creative process, "but are virtually inevitable to it"; and in any extended work of literature (he had the novel specifically in mind), the aesthetic effect "depends in large degree on intellectual power, upon the amount of recalcitrance of the material the mind works on, and upon the mind's success in mastering the large material" (*LI,* 276–77). In "Art and Fortune" he lists as one of the characteristics of the novel "the unabashed interest in ideas." Since the culture's novelists respond to involve certain congeries of ideas, "the great novels, far more often than we remember, deal explicitly with developed ideas" (*LI,* 243–44).

For Trilling, the principal function of literature is to meet the need "for mind to be applied to human life in its social and personal factuality and with the particular joy and goodwill of creativeness" (*SLS,* 245). He considered literature and life as inseparable, and his insistence on the cogency of literature accounts for his skepticism toward literature viewed as a self-justifying activity. It was natural, therefore, that he was drawn almost exclusively to the novel. He frankly acknowledges in his autobiographical lecture that his criticism took its direction from the novel and has a tendency "to occupy itself not with aesthetic questions, except secondarily, but rather with moral questions, with the questions raised by the experience of quotidian life and by the experience of culture and history" (*LD,* 228). He had a high estimation of the novel's capacity for social intelligence and questioned the assumption "which gives the priority of ideas to the philosopher and sees the movement of thought as always from the systematic thinker" (*LI,* 180). He insisted that the novel, better than all other expressions of human imagination, represents the mind in its subtlest and most complex operations and goes farther in combining the general with the particular, thought with feeling, and in generating ideas from a mass of contradictory details.

His conception of the nature and value of the novel derives naturally from his fundamental Arnoldian assumption that literature should be a criticism of life. Consequently, he valued verisimilitude, information about our life in culture, a strong sense of social fact, and close observation of shifting morals and manners. He thought the novel should give us "reasonably accurate news of the world" and tell us "the way things are" (*GF,* 98). Yet he advocated not a simple realism, but rather a portrait of reality shaped and articulated by a critical intellect, conditioned by a certain human impulse to know, accept, and control the way of the world. Most important of all the novel should have moral intensity, "for it is upon the degree and quality of moral intensity that all aesthetic considerations of the novel depend." But that moral intensity must not be narrow; it must include the delight and the gradual and eventual moral awareness that come from contemplating "the mere excess of irrelevant life" and "the impulse of sheer *performance*" (*GF,* 110, 112). "The novelist, in his ideal character," he says, "is the artist who is consumed with the desire to know how things really are, who entered into an elaborate romance with actuality. He is the artist of the conditioned, of the impingement of things upon spirit and of spirit upon things, and the success of his enterprise depends as much upon his awareness of things as upon his awareness of spirit" (*GF,* 100). This notion of the novelist's sense of internal life being concomitant with his sense of external life is a version of Trilling's belief that humans are responsible and conditioned. The novel should manifest this with inclusiveness and complexity. Its ability to do so constitutes the high standing and moral authority he attributed to it.

Such a conception of the novel implies a corresponding conception of the critic's task. Trilling believed that literature does not submit easily to the category of "aesthetic contemplative disinterestedness." Implicitly if not explicitly it makes assertions about human experience, and "if human experience—human danger and pain—is made the material of an artistic creation, the judgment that is directed upon the creation will involve important considerations of practicality and thus of cogency, relevance, appositeness, logicality, and truth." It may be by reason of prevaling accident rather than by reason of its essence, but "the judgment of literature is overtly and explicitly a moral and intellectual judgment. The cogency, the appositeness, the logicality, the *truth* of ideas must always be passed upon by literary criticism." Some critics set limits on or reject this mode of judgment; "they tell us that literature is an art like any other, and that the right experience of it shares this general characteristic of the aesthetic experience, that considerations of practicality—morality and truth—are essentially irrelevant. Alas! literature seems always to be telling the opposite" (*GF,* 145–46).

Trilling's persistent emphasis upon the priority of ideas in literature is easily misconstrued if his conception of mind is not taken into consideration. He was profoundly aware of the dangerous excesses of mind conceived restrictively as only rational intellect. This awareness pervades his criticism and constitutes one of its distinguishing characteristics. Repeatedly he decries the desiccation of spirit and moral contradictions that result from an allegiance to mind that excludes emotional complexity and human mystery. But he refused to disown mind because of its inadequate champions or for any other reason. As a thoroughgoing intellectual, his commitment to the values of the Enlightenment was firm: mind properly conceived, in his view, was mind possessing a dialectical quality and informed by imaginative reason. He borrowed the concept from Arnold and developed it his own way. Edward Joseph Shoben, Jr., explains that it combines three elements: "a rather severe and broadly informed rationality, a deliberate and habitual envisioning of alternatives . . . and an insistence on *feeling,* on the integral relationship of emotion and will to ideas."[64] Mind so conceived embodies wit, flexibility, moral perceptiveness, and a lively awareness of variousness and complexity. But it also generates order, and even a sense of hierarchy, and provides a basis for choices. Moreover, it is well adapted to objectivity, meaning the respect we give to the object as it exists apart from us or, in Arnold's term, the thing as it really is in itself. It represents an ideal mode of attention and leads to the realization of one's "best self," another Arnoldian phrase.

Trilling's own concept of mind is expressed in his description of Keats's concept. In this regard as well as in others, "The Poet as Hero: Keats in His Letters" *(OS)* functions almost as a Trilling credal statement and defines the bases of his criticism of modern culture. Keats, he says, did not suppose "that mind was an entity different in kind from and hostile to the sensations and emotions. Rather, mind came into being when the sensations and emotions were checked by external resistance or by conflict with each other, when, to use the language of Freud, the pleasure principle is confronted by the reality principle" (*OS,* 27). The reality principle was very strong in Keats, says Trilling, and of course the same could be said for Trilling.

Denis Donoghue emphasizes the social nature of Trilling's concept of mind. Trilling's theme, he says, is the mutual bearing of mind and society: "Society is never represented as a mere aggregate of philistines; mind is never represented as if its freedom were absolute and its activity unconditioned. The happiest situation is one in which spirit and matter, self and circumstance, make a harmony together and mind acknowledges its responsibility to society." Mind, almost by definition, is for him a social thing. He conceives it, therefore, "as the distinctively human attribute, the disinterested act of intelligence propelled by the sense of experience held in common . . . the power used by 'a man speaking to men' about the continuities of shared experience in the hope of understanding it."[65] Donoghue suggests that Trilling used the terminology of mind rather than imagination as a reaction against the extreme rhetoric of imagination found in the main tradition of European romanticism. The idiom of mind was more congenial to Trilling than the idiom of genius and imagination "because mind could be translated into practical terms and put to work in society; imagination and genius could not be put to work, or could be only indirectly and in forms too wayward to be trusted."[66] Trilling was inclined to judge mind by its results.

In his preoccupation with the novel and particularly the novel that brings mind to bear on society, Trilling's conservatism is most apparent. His essays are filled with nostalgic backward glances to the nineteenth century when novelists dealt unabashedly and significantly with ideas and the educated class gave serious attention to the best of its literature. "In the nineteenth century, in this country as in Europe, literature underlay every activity of mind" (*LI,* 91). He longed for such a situation, and a primary motivation in his criticism was to restore it in some measure by demonstrating the impact of literary ideas on modern culture. He was inclined to believe that the disappearance of serious ideas in the novel was symptomatic of a general intellectual decline in our culture. But, as many have argued, his was essentially a nineteenth-century conception of the novel, lacking the breadth and flexibility to adapt to the perplexing variety characteristic of recent trends in the novel. His prediction that "the novel of the next decades will deal in a very explicit way with ideas" (*LI,* 256) simply revealed his conservative hopes and in fact proved embarrassingly wide of the mark.

His concern with mind applied to social reality as the richest source of literary achievement and his emphasis on the novel had their cost. He was never comfortable with poetry apart from the degree to which he could bring poetic expression into the realm of ideas. He wrote perceptively about the moral dimensions of poets like Keats, Wordsworth, and Arnold, but had little interest in the aesthetic workings of their poems. The case of Keats is characteristic: he was attracted to Keats's letters and character rather than his poetry, to Keats the thinker rather than Keats the singer: "Keats was nothing if not a man of ideas" (*OS,* 4).

The single substantial essay on a poem during these middle years, "The Immortality Ode" in *The Liberal Imagination,* is content-oriented and has evoked the criticism that Trilling fails "to distinguish Wordsworth's mode from other modes of moral instruction" and he "detaches the sentiments of the Ode from the only medium in which they can live, the medium of their language."[67] As was mentioned already, Trilling confided to Allen Ginsberg his preference for prose, confessing that his relation to modern poetry was "largely academic and dutiful." In another letter to Ginsberg he admits that he is "uncertain and recessive" when he has to deal with poetry. And in still another he acknowledges that his tastes in poetry are "narrow and likely to be doctrinaire."[68] After remarking that Trilling "may have been a friend of literature but he was no fan of poetry," Mark Shechner perceptively explains that obviously the novel, "with its vistas and textures and examinations of character in society, suited his aesthetic and moral intuitions far better than did poetry, with its preference for the self in isolation and its traffic in those portions of the emotional life that lie below 'character,' that is, below scruples, judgment, values, reason, and the social instincts."[69]

Self and Society

One of Trilling's profoundest concerns was the nature of the individual self and its relationship with the context of society in which it exists. He believed that relationship to be fundamental and inescapable. It might be coercive or creative, starving or nourishing, but it is primary and indissolvable. He insisted that any view of human experience allowing the possibility for radical autonomy and unconditioned freedom for the individual self is an abstraction and falsification. Human fate is inescapably social, and though social life can be absurd and degrading, the human spirit must submit to it to exist at all. Consequently, throughout his criticism is this underlying question: What does this writer tell us about the constitution and potentialities of the self, its duties, and its sufferings in a world of conditioning circumstances?

This question is the particular and explicit focus of *The Opposing Self.* Most of the essays in this collection were written as introductions to books, but Trilling is correct in suggesting their interconnection. They treat literature since 1800 and the idea of self that constitutes its unifying principle. According to Trilling's preface, a new concept of self emerged at the end of the eighteenth century, its distinguishing characteristic being "its intense and adverse imagination of the culture in which it has its being." This "modern imagination of autonomy and delight, of surprise and elevation, of selves conceived in opposition to the general culture" he believed to be "a new idea in the world."

The Opposing Self carries forward the theme of *The Liberal Imagination* in a new phase. Borrowing a term from Jacques Maritain, Nathan A. Scott, Jr., calls that theme "angelism"—"that penchant for life in the angelic mode which is fostered by the passion for the clear and distinct idea." This inclination to insist that life be pure spirit, which Trilling thought was such a temptation in modern literary and intellectual life, inspires, says Scott, a "tendency to conceive the ideal posture of the self in relation to 'the conditioned' as one of an 'opposition' so radical as to entail an essentially angelic aspiration."[70] Just as some have accepted the title *The Liberal Imagination* as intended in an entirely positive sense, there are those who see "the opposing self" as the unqualified hero of *The Opposing Self.* This is inaccurate and misleading because of Trilling's important reservations regarding the opposing self. He viewed self and society in a perennial dialectical relationship in which neither term can or ought to yield to the other. The first essay, the very important one on Keats, makes the nature of the relationship clear. He admires Keats because of his firm grip on the essential fact that the destiny of the self is always to confront the difficult and limiting actualities of circumstances: "He has brought his two knowledges face to face, the knowledge of the world of circumstance, of death and cancer, and the knowledge of the world of self, of spirit and creation, and the delight in them. Each seems a whole knowledge considered alone; each is but a half-knowledge when taken with the other; both together constitute a truth" (*OS,* 37).

Bringing the two knowledges together as Keats did is the process of "soul making"—the self creates itself in confrontation with conditioning circumstances. Throughout his career, Trilling was preoccupied with this process, which accounts for his lasting interest in manners, morals, and the commonplace elements of culture. He was, in fact, more interested in self-construction than in self-knowledge. After quoting these lines from Arnold—"Resolve to be thyself: and know, that he / Who finds himself, loses his misery"—he emphasizes approvingly that "the advice is not *know* thyself but *be* thyself" (*MA,* 27). How to *be* was the essential question for Trilling, particularly in *The Opposing Self.* He used the phrase "the sentiment of being" to designate the desired consciousness of one's own existence. By this he meant "such energy as contrives that the center {of the self} shall hold, that the circumference of the self keep unbroken, that the person be an integer, impenetrable, perdurable, and autonomous in being if not in action" (*SA,* 92). He undoubtedly had in mind a quality existing in some measure in his own personal experience, what Diana Trilling describes as "an undefined feeling of personal worth, some secret quality of being to which he could give no name but on which he could ultimately rely" (*SLS,* 413).

The proper sentiment of being requires of the self a lively sensory awareness of its surrounding environment, a continuous interaction with it, not on the level of abstraction, but in commonplace details: simple objects, domestic matters, family ties, trivial social interaction. Cultivating the ability to struggle and the capacity for pleasure on this level produces emotional depth and complexity of self. So fortified, the self can better cope with the tragic realities of human life, specifically, as he argues in the case of Keats, with the problem of evil. Such a self is not debilitated or annihilated by the coercive pressure of the culture. Jeffrey Robinson suggests that ordinary things and events function for Trilling as "a kind of modern sublime. They never lose their existence as opposing, 'intractable' forces and realities, but they may become occasions for a freedom within and for the mind to embrace a large, more difficult but truer reality."[71] The essays on Keats, Wordsworth, and Howells display a similar progression of thought: involvement with mundane circumstances leads to the achievement of a strong sense of self or sentiment of being, which in turn enhances the capacity to cope with evil. In contrast to such nineteenth-century figures, the modern literary mind, he says in the essay on Howells, is interested in "the rare and strange"; family ties are dissolving and "we are not responsive to the common, the immediate, the familiar, and the vulgar elements in life" (*OS,* 77). The conditioning circumstances we do respond to "are the ones we ourselves make, or over which we have control, which is to say conditions as they are virtually spirit, as they deny the idea of *the conditioned.* Somewhere in our mental constitution is the demand for life as pure spirit" (*OS,* 79).

Much of the book is summed up in his admiration for Tolstoy's awareness that the human spirit is always at the mercy of the actual and trivial. Concluding the essay on *Anna Karenina,* he notes that author's "passionate sense that the actual and trivial are of the greatest importance" and at the same time "his certainty that they are not of final importance." This, Trilling insists, is not a modest sort of knowledge: "to comprehend unconditioned spirit is not so very hard, but there is no knowledge rarer than the understanding of spirit as it exists in the inescapable conditions which the actual and trivial make for it" (*OS*, 65–66).

A firm and vibrant sentiment of self, then, is Trilling's touchstone of health and value, but since it is achieved only within the social context, it must not be allowed to triumph over the sentiment of society. His complicated awareness of the conflicting claims of self and society, his understanding that one must be in culture but not entirely of culture and that both total submission to it and alienation from it equally diminish human life, is the source from which much of his thought proceeds. He naturally looked to literature for help when self was in danger of being overwhelmed by society or culture: "The function of literature, through all its mutations, has been to make us aware of the particularity of selves, and of the high authority of the self in its quarrel with its society and culture" (*BC*, 89). But although nothing is more fundamental in Trilling's thought than the primacy and privilege it grants to the self, his partisanship, as Tom Samet explains, "was nevertheless of a very special sort—cautious, ambivalent, freighted with misgiving and hedged about by every available qualification. For Trilling could not conceive of the self as something anterior to culture or entirely separable from it—something 'liberated,' as it were, from a conditioning matrix of objects and institutions and others."[72]

Trilling's criticism during the fifties was primarily concerned with determining the proper balance between the individual and the culture, and Freud was his chief ally in this endeavor, particularly the Freud of *Civilization and Its Discontents* and *Beyond the Pleasure Principle.* Freud confirmed Trilling's conviction that a complex blending of culture and biology forms the bedrock of natural truths. While some find Freud's biological determinism pessimistic, Trilling found it a bracing and possibly liberating idea in that it allows that at least some part of man is safe from determination by culture. The religious mind looks to a supernatural realm for such possibility of freedom. Trilling's thoroughly secular orientation influenced him to seek it in Freud's view of man's biological resistance to culture.

The resigned, tragic stance Trilling assumed under the influence of Freud has disturbed liberal critics who interpret it as uncertainty, or quietism, or even as reactionary—an ambivalent acceptance of the given in society and the biological in human life. Mark Krupnick, for example, complains that "for all his biological self-certitude, however, Trilling's opposing self does very little opposing. He stands opposed not to particular social evils but to the human condition itself."[73] This is a misunderstanding of what Trilling meant by the opposing self. The self he described is not in opposition to social injustice or political oppression in the usual sense; it is in opposition to the force of any cultural idea that would undercut its familiar human ground, the conditioning, soul-making circumstances that along with pain and struggle bring felicity and beauty as well as compensation for a tragic reality. The quietism he praised in Wordsworth and obviously cultivated in himself was, as he insisted, "not in the least a negation of life, but, on the contrary, an affirmation of life" (*OS,* 115).

Most of Trilling's important essays of the fifties were occupied with biography rather than with the close analysis of literary texts. He was searching for exemplars, heroes of thought, whose heroism consists of a wise and balanced awareness of the equally authoritative claims of individual autonomy and the conditioning circumstances of an essentially tragic human reality. They are, in Mark Shechner's phrase, "mature adversaries of culture."[74] Arnold and Freud preside in this pantheon, of course, accompanied by Keats, Wordsworth, Forster, James, Orwell, Mill, Austen, and others. Admittance to this honored group required meeting the qualification Keats so admirably fulfilled: "It is, indeed, of the very nature of his whole intellectual and moral activity that he should hold in balance the reality of self and the reality of circumstance" (*OS,* 37).

Chapter Five
The Last Decade

The Adversary Culture

During the forties and fifties, his most fruitful period, Trilling's writing displayed its best attributes: a courteous, reasonable tone, a balanced intelligence, and a graceful flexible style. In these years he combined clarity of thought and purpose with full faith in literature as an instrument of social and moral good. His stance was that of the enlightened humanist making the best of the past relevant and meaningful to the present in hope of perpetuating it. The nineteenth-century novel in particular provided him his best models because it focused on the social fabric in which human relationships are established. He thought the great novelists of the last century were aware of how the spirit is hedged and shaped by circumstance. They realized that the price of civilization is high but its rewards are great and its opposite is fruitless barbarism. In their work the ultimate desirability of civilization is unquestioned.

At the same time Trilling was aware of these positive elements in the nineteenth-century novel, he recognized their absence in many twentieth-century novels. At first he tried to suggest ways for modern novelists to take advantage of the earlier tradition, but gradually he became disturbed that modern literature seemed to provide so few examples of literature promoting moral good. With its emphasis on the self in an adversary relationship to society, modern literature appeared to question civilization itself. This alarmed Trilling because, from his secular perspective, the social relationship is the only source of obligation and authority. Modern literature had become divisive and sullen on the one hand or merely playful or whimsical on the other, and its truculent devaluation of traditional social and ethical values demonstrated that it might provide only flimsy support to moral awareness. Increasingly his Arnoldian faith in literature as a social stabilizer was subjected to some very harsh tests, and at some point he began a circuitous, perhaps only partly conscious, investigation of origins, a consideration of how and why modern works became what they are. Much of his work after 1950 should be read as a transcript of discomforts occasioned by an actively radical literature in a mind for which the idea of society was of ultimate concern—a mind, moreover, inveterately preoccupied with consequences and responsibility. During his last decade, Trilling began to unravel some of the more devastating implications of his own early arguments about the "adversary culture." During the sixties, his criticism underwent a change as he reexamined the traditional defense of humane letters. His answers to his own implicit and continuing question as to the function and value of literature began to display a marked shift in emphasis and a sense of alarm. He turned increasingly away from specific consideration of literary works to a general critique of the modern temperament.

Delmore Schwartz perceived as early as 1953 that Trilling had "the most serious misgivings about the extremism, the bias and the methods of all modernist authors."[1] Trilling was disturbed at the time by this charge, but it was largely justified, as his last decade demonstrates. He admired the great modernist writers, but, with the exception of Eliot, he felt no affinity with them. But he could not ignore modern literature, as uncongenial and intrusive as he might find it to be. For one thing, he was associated for many years with *Partisan Review,* which, according to William Phillips, one of its longtime editors, sanctioned the idea—"perhaps the most powerful cultural idea of the century—that there existed an all-but-incomparable generation of modern masters who represented for our time the highest reaches of the imagination."[2] In other words, his intellectual environment as a New York writer accentuated the priority of modern authors. Moreover, his own flexibility of mind would not permit him to ignore the writers of his age. There was something formidable and exigent about the great modernists that aroused his sense of duty. To ignore such genius was impossible. A year prior to his death, he recalled what had been his posture toward modernism. Before most of that literature, he said, "I stood puzzled, abashed, and a little queasy; I was at least as much alienated from it as I was from the culture to which it opposed itself. . . . I took the view, pious and dull enough, that the advanced art of one's own age cannot possibly be irrelevant to one's own experience and that one is under the virtually moral obligation to keep one's consciousness open to it."[3] This resigned sense of obligation contrasts sharply with the affectionate fascination he manifested toward authors of the past century.

In view of his Arnoldian values and his firm commitment to the humanistic tradition, Trilling's antipathy to modern literature is not surprising. But it must be remembered that his discomfort with it was a form of respect. He was fully aware of the force and seriousness of its attack on hard-earned human order. And although greatly distressed by the adversary culture, he knew that meaningful intellectual and critical endeavor necessarily entails adversarial relationships. The achievement of selfhood and individual autonomy were always at the center of his intellectual life, and he realized that such achievement often meant going against the grain of culture. What worried him more than modern literature itself was the tendency of middle-class intellectuals to domesticate and trivialize it with bland acceptance. The later essays frequently manifest his discouragement with the way hard-won achievements of the opposing self were being mass-produced and sold in cheap packages such as the counterculture of the sixties, which he once referred to as "modernism in the streets."[4] On the one hand, he welcomed the liberating thrust of the moderns and sympathized with their aggressive advocacy of a more richly realized self; but on the other, he was alarmed at the way this adversary impulse had become conventionalized. The battle of the opposing self had paradoxically ended in an unnerving, unseemly triumph that generated a culture of its own, which in turn posed a renewed threat to the self.

Suspicious of modern literature but obliged to cope with it, Trilling during his last decade was faced with the dilemma of reconciling two divergent convictions. First, that great literature benefits man individually and socially by stimulating and extending his moral imagination and enlarging his awareness of himself and his necessary connection with his fellows. Second, that modern literature, though possessing genius, has divorced morality from imagination and denied the validity of the social connection, and consequently may be harmful. Irving Howe remarks that Trilling exposed a dualism of response many literary people feel but few can state: "There is the Trilling who teaches, writes about, and defines himself culturally through the modernist masters, writers of the oblique, perverse, complex, problematic. This Trilling responds to the violence, the moral chaos proudly thrust forward, the refusal of simple virtues or verities, the negation of worn or indeed any certainties, all of which we know to be the glory of our literature." But another Trilling is heard, "a little weary with the suave virtuosity of the first one, more and more ironic toward the performance of ironies that has become the set-piece of the 'advanced' critic, falling back with some didactic bravado on the moral assurances of the 19th-century writers. This second Trilling seems to wonder—he cannot suppress the heresy, and then finds relief in venting it, since that defines *his* authenticity—

whether the whole modernist enterprise will turn out to have been a brilliant detour of Western culture from which, at great cost, we may have to find a path of return."[5]

Beyond Culture (1965) marks a significant and deeply felt change in Trilling's thought. It was not an abrupt change, however, for it had been taking shape gradually for years. From our vantage point, an early and persistent uneasiness with modernism is clearly discernible in his writing. The pattern revealed in Trilling's development is paradoxical. He was a humanist believer that man fulfills his highest potential in society, with literature serving as a principal edifying and socializing agency; yet nowhere in his culture did he find society fostering the fruits of civilization he admired, and literature, rather than strengthening social bonds, was assuming an increasingly adversarial stance toward society. Eventually he was moved to express doubts about the edifying value of literature.

In the preface to *Beyond Culture,* he admits to being himself rather surprised by his new, heretical view of literature. As a result of confronting modern literature, particularly in confronting particular authors and works with students, he had done an about-face from his original Arnoldian position. This is not to say that his allegiance to Arnold had lessened but rather that a new kind of literature had emerged unsuited to Arnold's assumptions. He notes with an exclamation mark how far Arnold's ideal of the modern is removed from our present sense of modernity and from our modern literature (*BC,* 14). He admits that even since 1950, when he described the novel as the most effective instrument for educating people in moral realism, the novel "has undergone a mutation which manifestly makes my old characterization of it obsolete" (*LD,* 141). *Beyond Culture* portrays modernism as a seductive force so powerful and authoritative in its blurring of older moral distinctions that almost nothing can withstand it. Many reviewers of the book complained about the astringent tone toward modernism without recognizing the magnitude of the intellectual decisions Trilling was facing. He was calling into question what modern aesthetics takes as self-evident: "that art yields more truth than any other intellectual activity." In other words, he was questioning the epistemological assumption that creative imagination and art rather than reason and morality are the best guides to authentic human existence. He suggests in his preface that, as a matter of fact, "art does not always tell the truth or the best kind of truth and does not always point out the right way, that it can even generate falsehood and habituate us to it" (*BC,* xiv). As early as the fifties, he had remarked in an aside that "No one has yet paid attention to the anti-catharsis, the generally anti-hygienic effect of bad serious art, the stimulation it gives to all one's neurotic tendencies, the literal, physically-felt depression it induces" (*GF,* 99). His doubts about the edifying effects of art grew during his final years, and he found himself asking "whether that wonderful Victorian confidence in the educative, moralizing power of art has been justified or if it can be accepted simply and without qualification."[6] "What is the basis of our society's belief that art is so important?" he asked. "What do we expect of it? Only good, it seems. I am quite open to the idea that art can produce bad effects as well as good ones, even that what might be called good art can produce bad effects. . . . I would like to hear why, apart from its usefulness as entertainment, art should be supported."[7] He seemed not unhappy with Rousseau's objections to literature as a principal agent of man's corruption as he describes them in *Sincerity and Authenticity* (58–59). He worried about the way art interposes itself between us and experience: "I think it does in the way Rousseau thought it did; it keeps us from looking at the object directly, it keeps us from experiencing things directly."[8] Furthermore, he was alarmed by the enormous moral credence, tantamount to religious faith, that the adversary culture places in literature, particularly in light of the proliferation of art that has transformed it into a trivial commodity.

In *Beyond Culture* and other essays of the last decade, he presents modernism as a kind of demon god that is rarely met "on its own fierce terms." Of modern criticism as he and others have practiced it, he says, "It has taught us how to read certain books; it has not taught us how to engage them"; it has done little more than instruct us in "an intelligent passivity before the beneficent aggression of literature. Attributing to literature virtually angelic powers, it has passed the word to readers of literature that the one thing you do not do when you meet an angel is wrestle with him" (*BC,* 200).

Like "the liberal imagination" and "the opposing self," "beyond culture" is another of Trilling's complex and ambiguous phrases, possessing both positive and negative implications. Self-realization requires of individuals a certain transcendence of their culture, but the modern impulse to go beyond culture in the sense of aggressively rejecting society in pursuit of the autonomous self he viewed with alarm. Moreover, he found this impulse self-deluding because it had resulted in an adversary culture with its own pressures for conformity. Consequently, literary art can no longer free us from the tyranny of culture because it constitutes itself a culture with tyrannical tendencies. A narrowly aesthetic culture is not enough. We need values beyond those of literature and art and thus need to get beyond the adversary culture. In another of its senses, "beyond culture" means getting beyond modern culture and appreciating the past. Trilling always extolled the benefits of getting beyond one's culture by learning of another and thereby seeing one's own more objectively. And finally, woven into all of this, is his vague but enduring longing for a source of authority beyond culture. He could not look for it in religion and therefore turned to his beloved Freud. The superego functions, says Trilling, "to lead us to imagine that there is a sanction beyond the culture, that there is a place from which the culture may be judged and rejected" (*BC,* 101).

During his last years, Trilling was preoccupied with questions like these: What is happening to the self in our culture? What are the possibly undesirable effects of an influential modern literature? What are the consequences of an overly busy and ingenious criticism with little concern with literature's relation to life? What are we doing when we set out to "teach" literature?

His answers took the form of a cluster of ideas that shapes and unifies the writing of his last decade. First was the idea that modern literature is animated by a kind of moral aggression and acts deliberately and purposively in opposition to society. "Any historian of the literature of the modern age will take virtually for granted the adversary intention, the actually subversive intention, that characterizes modern writing" (*BC,* x). Though it appears primarily concerned with aesthetics, its formal gestures imply intentions that, taken seriously, change behavior and values. And though it appears indifferent or hostile to religion, "no literature has ever been so intensely spiritual as ours" (*BC,* 8). He had in mind the uncompromising demands of the energetic modern self for radical autonomy, the angelism with which it insists upon direct access to spirit and resists conditions and circumstances—"stupid literal matter." He had been captivated by E. M. Forster's phrase "only connect"—meaning connect "the prose and the passion" and be aware that man is neither beast nor angel. He found in modern literature the avowed principle *"only disconnect!"* (*LD,* 36). "Our modern piety is preoccupied by the ideal of the autonomous self, or at least of the self as it seeks autonomy in its tortured dream of metaphysical freedom" (*BC,* 178). His distrust of such angelism was instinctive because of its attendant devaluation of man's life in society. As Denis Donoghue explains: "The notion of escaping from society into a state of ostensibly unconditioned spirit was uniquely disturbing to him precisely because he did not feel immune to its force and because it placed at risk the only source of obligation and authority he could regard as having any hope of success in the world [i.e., society]: if it failed, failure was complete."[9]

A second idea is that the mystique of unpleasure is a distinctive type of modern spirituality. Contemporary aesthetic culture, he asserts, is antagonistic to the principle of pleasure (*BC,* 63) and experiences art through anxiety rather than pleasure (*LD,* 123). "The imagination of felicity is difficult for us to exercise. We feel that it is a betrayal of our awareness of our world of pain, that it is politically inappropriate" (*BC,* 45). For the modern temper, "the disgust with the specious good of pleasure serves as the ground for the affirmation of spiritual freedom" (*BC,* 66). Following Freud's notion that ungratified drives turn destructive, Trilling suggests that modern literature distorts the impulse toward pleasure—accepted and nurtured in former times, notably by Keats and Wordsworth, for whom the principle of pleasure was the principle of reality (*BC,* 57)—and replaces it with the death wish. This cult of unpleasure perpetuates conventionalized sentiments of alienation and bitterness that go unexamined and untested by actual experience.

A third recurrent idea, most fully developed in "Art, Will, and Necessity," is that will, which was a central and controlling topic in the psychological and ethical theory of the nineteenth century, is no longer valued in our high culture (*LD,* 130–31). This is largely due to the autonomous self's fatal indifference to limitation, conditioning circumstance, and necessity in its quest for spiritual freedom. He has in mind in this context will as "that element of character which we mobilize to meet the demands of necessity—it is the *will* of that now discredited phrase *will-power.*" It has been replaced by a narcissistic will, "the will of the undeveloped ego, unresponsive to necessity" (*LD,* 146–47). One need not be deeply instructed in the contradictions of the unconscious, he says, to understand that the surest negation of actual willpower is the fantasy of the omnipotent will characteristic of modern culture (*LD,* 137). Will detached from necessity results in "weightlessness" and a severe diminishment of life's purpose and meaning. "The sense of commitment, the sense of actuality, the sense of weightiness—gravity it used to be called—is going at the behest of a feeling for autonomy. That wonderful word which is so popular in our culture is a very dangerous word, indeed."[10]

A fourth central idea is that our culture is marked by an "uneasy or ambivalent or actually disaffected relation to mind" (*LD,* 117). This is the controlling theme of "Mind in the Modern World," the first Thomas Jefferson Lecture in the Humanities, presented under the auspices of the National Endowment for the Humanities in 1972. Trilling argues that in our time "the social compensations for the sacrifice of personal autonomy which mind is presumed to exact have been drastically devalued, and, as a consequence, resentment of the authority of mind has grown to the point of becoming a virtually political emotion." Furthermore, mind is now impeached for its commitment to the ideal of objectivity: "What has been called the myth of objective consciousness is held to be pre-eminently responsible for the dehumanizing tendency of our culture" (*LD,* 120). The adversary culture values highest those things experienced without intervention of rational thought and views irrationalism as a hallmark of authenticity (*LD,* 123). Nevertheless, this same culture tends to turn such experience into ideas, "as witness the present ideational and ideological status of sex, violence, madness, and art itself" (*BC,* xv). Therefore, Trilling suggests, the adversary culture needs to be brought under the analyzing and evaluating power of rational scrutiny.

Though the central concerns and attitudes of his last decade are essentially those underlying his entire career, his focus on the adversary culture caused them to be more clearly defined and explicit, and also caused some ironic shifts in emphasis. The burden of his polemic during the forties and fifties had been an antagonism toward energized will and intellect and a sympathy with the opposing self. In his last years he was promoting will and mind, now taken in different senses, and roundly condemning the autonomous self. His position was closer than ever to that of Irving Babbitt and Paul Elmer More, the most notable Arnoldian humanists of the first decades of the century. "Civilization, at bottom, rests on the recognition of the fact that man shows his true liberty by resisting impulse, and not by yielding to it, that he grows in the perfection proper to his own nature not by throwing off but by taking on limitations."[11] This is Babbitt speaking, but the statement would fit appropriately in several of Trilling's later essays.

Literature and Education

Trilling's devotion to education was deep and abiding. He resisted every temptation to abandon the classroom, and his criticism itself was informed by a spirit of teaching. His interest in literature from the beginning was centered in its educative function, and he acknowledged that most of his education was provided by literature, particularly the novel. This deep-seated and perennial concern with literature and education is clearly manifest in his final decade by his publication of two textbooks and three major essays devoted exclusively to questions of teaching and education. He was also the coeditor of *The Oxford Anthology of English Literature* (1973).

The Experience of Literature (1967), an anthology of literature designed primarily for introductory courses, is unusual, not in its choice of representative selections, but in its numerous commentaries. Each story and play and certain of the poems are accompanied by brief essays. These essays were collected separately for the Uniform Edition of Trilling's works and actually constitute, next to *Speaking of Literature and Society,* the largest collection of his essays: *Prefaces to The Experience of Literature.* The commentaries were not intended to "usurp or circumscribe the teacher's function," but, as a matter of fact, they did, and the anthology was a victim of its own success: many teachers felt Trilling left them too little to add.

Trilling says in the introduction: "No special theory of literature or method of criticism informs what I have written." Regarding this statement, his publisher, in the foreword to *Prefaces to The Experience of Literature,* wryly remarks, "This is the disclaimer from the author of *The Liberal Imagination, Beyond Culture,* and *The Opposing Self!*" And of course the commentaries constitute an encyclopedia of the author's characteristic concerns and attitudes: a constitutional awareness of complexity; references to Freud, Arnold, and Keats's letters; a rigorously secular perspective; a focus on social, political, cultural, moral, and biographical concerns; a pervasive historical sense combined with an inveterate tendency to justify past attitudes and values to contemporary readers; a preoccupation with death and the tragic vision; a content-oriented treatment of poetry; and so on. Trilling's disclaimer is not entirely disingenuous, however, for he actually believed his method to be broad and eclectic. And an anthology with such commentaries was an appropriate undertaking for him because he was essentially a teacher and explainer as opposed to a performer, scholar, propagandist, or theorist. But even so, it is difficult to suppress the suspicion that this anthology with commentaries was partly intended to counter current trends in criticism and the teaching of literature. The title itself provides a clue: it is the *experience* of literature whose value he is reaffirming, recognizing that literature as a classroom subject of instruction is not always an experience but more often an occasion for explication and objective knowledge. Furthermore, the experience, while private and autonomous, is ultimately communal and therefore a social enhancement.

Literary Criticism: An Introductory Reader (1970) is the usual sort of survey of criticism, beginning with Plato and ending with Susan Sontag. Its special interest lies in its preface, treating the place of criticism in literary education, and its introduction (reprinted in *The Last Decade*), "What Is Criticism?" His attitude toward the teaching of criticism, expressed or implied here, is ambivalent. On the one hand, he is uneasy that criticism has become too busy, brilliant, and influential: "Like much else in modern culture, criticism [has] become plethoric and hyperactive, taking on something of the aspect of a fashion or an exciting new sport" (*LC,* vii). On the other, he suggests that American thought about education has been misguided by "progressive" doctrine, producing "an antagonism to generalization and speculative abstraction and a tenderness for what is called 'affective education' in contradistinction to 'cognitive education' " (*LC,* ix). With his strongly rational temperament, he of course favored cognitive education: "The fear that the affective life will be desiccated and made less sincere and authentic by such cognitive activity is groundless" (*LC,* x). The study of criticism is a way to engage young minds in speculation and rational discourse.

"What Is Criticism?," although ostensibly an objective overview of the question, is clearly a reaffirmation of the humanistic tradition to which Trilling subscribed. While conceding that "at the present time the idea that literature is to be judged by its moral effect has virtually no place in critical theory" (*LD,* 67), he insists that in actual critical practice it has considerable vitality. He goes on to argue that "the intention of judgment is a salient motive of all critical theories" (*LD,* 72). The emphasis on Arnold's admonition "to see the object as in itself it really is," on the concept of culture, on the relevance of biography, and on the conditioned nature of literature and criticism as well as life—all these are Trilling hallmarks. A statement in the concluding paragraph tellingly reveals an attitude that, always part of his response to literature, became more pronounced in his later years: "there are times when criticism seems beside the point of literature and it is literature beyond the reach of criticism that we want, just as there are times when literature itself seems beside the point of life and it is life itself beyond the reach of literature that we want" (*LD,* 99). Although in this context—an essay encouraging the study of criticism—

he plays down this notion, he nevertheless believed it. He was fond of quoting Keats's statement that poetry "is not so fine a thing as philosophy—For the same reason that an eagle is not so fine a thing as a truth" (e.g., *BC,* 26, 202). And in the essay on Jane Austen left unfinished at his death, he admits to having held "the primitive belief that there really was such a thing as life itself, which I did not want interfered with by literature or by the ingenuities of academic criticism" (*LD,* 207).

In addition to preparing these two textbooks during the sixties, Trilling evidenced his preoccupation with literature and education in three major essays: "On the Teaching of Modern Literature" *(BC),* "The Two Environments: Reflections on the Study of English" *(BC),* and "The Uncertain Future of the Humanistic Educational Ideal" *(LD).*

Although he taught modern literature at Columbia for many years, he never undertook to do so without misgivings and "never taught it with an undivided mind." And this uneasiness increased rather than diminished with the passage of time (*BC,* 4, 7). It was less a matter of doubts about the literature itself than about the educational propriety of its being studied in college. He was reluctant to teach modern literature for a number of reasons. One was that he highly valued the study of another culture, which he thought produced breadth, perspective, and objectivity. He had in mind past cultures and particularly those of the preceding century. In his estimation, a sense of the past was extremely important, and he lamented "the ever-diminishing place that history is given in the curriculums of our schools and colleges" (*LD,* 105). He feared that modern literature, rather than leading beyond one's own culture, simply indoctrinated one into it. Rather than allowing the self "to detach itself from its bondage to the idols of the Marketplace, the Tribe, the Theatre, and even of the Cave," modern literature inverts this old ideal of humanistic education and sets up "the old idols in new forms of its own contrivance" (*BC,* 201–2).

A second reason he doubted the appropriateness of teaching modern literature in college is that such an enterprise accelerates the decline of the humanistic ideal of general education, "which insisted in the traditional humanistic way that the best citizen is the person who has learned from the great minds and souls of the past how beautiful reason and virtue are and how difficult to attain" (*LD,* 165). Events of the sixties alarmed him with how quickly that ideal could disappear from higher education, and he must have felt some complicity because of his teaching of modern literature. The classic defense of literary study, he pointed out, holds that "from the effect which the study of literature has upon the private sentiments of a student, there results, or can be made to result, an improvement in the intelligence, and especially the intelligence as it touches the moral life" (*BC,* 184). He doubted, given the nature of modern literature, that the classic justification of literary study still had force. At a conference on the Educated Person in the Contemporary World a year before his death, he stated flatly his conclusion that "our society will tend increasingly to alienate itself from the humanistic educational ideal" (*LD,* 161).

A third reason he was reluctant to teach modern literature is incidental but nevertheless not to be discounted. It had to do with the personal force and moral aggressiveness of that literature, which necessitated, he felt, that the teacher eventually, after all the discussion of formal matters, must bear personal testimony: "He must use whatever authority he may possess to say whether or not a work is true; and if not, why not; and if so, why so. He can do this only at considerable cost to his privacy" (*BC,* 8). This cost was especially dear for a temperament such as Trilling's, which prized cool detachment, exquisite tolerance for opposing views, and the vague comfort of a wise negative capability.

A fourth reason for his uneasiness was his suspicion that "when modern literature is brought into the classroom, the subject being taught is betrayed by the pedagogy of the subject." As universities have liberalized themselves and turned "their imperialistic gaze upon what is called Life Itself," the feeling has grown that every experience needs the validation of some established intellectual discipline, "with the result that experience loses much of its personal immediacy for us and becomes part of an accredited societal activity" (*BC,* 9). University study, in other words, alters and institutionalizes the experience of modern literature and "tends to accelerate the process by which the radical and subversive work becomes the classic work." The passion and subversiveness of modern literature become domesticated and even trivialized in the classroom, especially when the literary work is considered only as a structure of words without regard to the author's social and personal will. Exam questions make such good sense that "the young person who answers them can never again know the force and terror of what has been communicated to him by the works he is being examined on" (*BC,* 10–11). His teaching impressed him with "the readiness of the students to engage in the process that we might call the socialization of the anti-social, or the acculturation of the anti-cultural, or the legitimization of the subversive" (*BC,* 23). Feeling that his irony in treating these matters had not been fully recognized, he added an addendum to the preface of the second edition of *Beyond Culture* making explicit his alarm at the hospitality shown to "radical and subversive art by the established and respectable agencies of our culture. To be explicit: I regard with misgivings the growing affinity between the university and the arts" (*SLS,* 407).

Finally, the most significant reason for his reservations about teaching modern literature was his belief that when that literature is taken unexamined, as he felt his students were taking it, it loses its formidable power to free and challenge the self. Moreover, it fails even to give pleasure of the kind that releases the self, momentarily at least, from the sordidness of the mundane and provides consolation in the face of uncertainties and fear. It actually does just the opposite, diminishing and circumscribing the self and inhibiting its freedom of expression by promoting conformity to the adversary culture. Trilling became increasingly convinced that literature strongly stressing autonomy, primacy of self, cultivation of self in all its untrammeled authenticity, paradoxically contributes to a false or inadequate sense of self. Because of its intense examination and isolation of self, its fierce rejection of society and insistence on the autonomy of self, modern literature's effect on students (if they receive it uncritically) is to free them from middle-class concepts of duty, honor, social responsibility, and ultimately the allegiance to civilization itself. "Nothing is more characteristic of modern literature," says Trilling, "than its discovery and canonization of the primal, non-ethical energies" (*BC,* 17). Consequently, the teacher of literature, traditionally the defender of civilized values, might actually be subversive of his society and of civilization itself. Furthermore, since alienation is the dominant note in modern literature, the student, in order to be considered liberal and enlightened, must be alienated and hostile to traditional society. But this is not an act of conviction and courage; it is just being intellectually fashionable. "The literature itself is not trivial," Trilling emphasizes. "But there has grown out of this literature, or around it, a cultural environment which might well lead some serious teachers to think twice before undertaking to prepare their students to enter it" (*BC,* 198). Trilling's doubts about teaching modern literature, his suspicion that doing so meant a betrayal of society as well as of the literature itself, is epitomized by his striking metaphor of the abyss. He had asked his students "to look into the Abyss, and, both dutifully and gladly, they have looked into the Abyss, and the Abyss has greeted them with the grave courtesy of all objects of serious study, saying:

'Interesting, am I not? And *exciting,* if you consider how deep I am and what dread beasts lie at my bottom. Have it well in mind that a knowledge of me contributes materially to your being whole, or well-rounded men' " (*BC,* 24).

Sincerity and Authenticity

Sincerity and Authenticity (1972) is the published version of a series of lectures Trilling delivered at Harvard in the spring of 1970 during his 1969–70 appointment as Charles Eliot Norton Professor of Poetry. It is a synthesizing rather than an original effort. At the heart of these lectures is the central anxiety expressed in so many variations during his late years: the unsettling notion that modern literature encourages the disregard of conditioning realities and the tearing of the social fabric; and by eroding social ties, however flawed, and by elevating individual autonomy and resentment of culture as essential conditions for achieving authenticity, it actually promotes a false or deficient sense of being. *Sincerity and Authenticity,* therefore, is not a new departure for Trilling in terms of themes or even texts cited, but it marks an attempt to understand modern literature more fully by viewing it as a manifestation of a larger historical transformation of the moral life during the past four hundred years. In its breadth, penetration, and historical perspective, it serves as a kind of summing up of his views of modern culture.

Trilling was impelled to come to terms with modern literature. He wanted somehow to find an approach to it that would allow him to maintain his Arnoldian conviction that literature promotes and clarifies the moral life. Yet, on every hand, and particularly in the youth culture of the sixties, he found evidence to the contrary. And as he probed the relationship of culture and literature, he saw that the aspects of modern literature that controverted his humanistic convictions were a natural outgrowth of a shift in the values animating the moral life, a shift he delineated as a movement from sincerity to authenticity. The impulsion toward a moral justification of modern literature in tension with historical evidence that literature may have outlived its moral usefulness is the implicit dialectic of *Sincerity and Authenticity* and accounts for its tentativeness and ambiguity in assertion.

The book resists summary because it lacks a clear linear progession of argument. Major motifs come into focus and then fade in circuitous variations. For the most part, judgments are meticulously avoided or expressed so cautiously and subtly as to give the impression of ambivalence or self-contradiction. According to Marianne Gilbert Barnaby, who has provided one of the more illuminating discussions of the book, it reveals "a highly cultivated mind on a restless and intricate search for certainties that ever elude it."[12] But seen in its simplest terms, the book describes the way a new concept of self emerged at the end of the eighteenth century as an antithesis to that which had developed in the Renaissance. The earlier view of self had emerged with the concept of society itself as a thing clearly recognized and discussed. Centered in the idea of sincerity, this Renaissance conception of self viewed the sincere man as a vital constituent of society, sincerity being inextricably linked with public and political considerations. For the sincere man, art served an essentially pedagogic function: to teach people to fulfill themselves in moral life within the community, while at the same time delighting and consoling them in their efforts. The later concept of self, suspicious of the limiting and coercive aspects of society, turned to authenticity as a desideratum in place of sincerity. The ground of reality for this view was not society but exclusively the self, which achieves freedom in alienation from society. Art for those who prized authenticity lost its value as a source of ethical truth or consolation and became valued instead as an agent of spiritual self-realization necessitating a painful abandonment of social norms. These two conceptions of self, kept in balance, form a complex idea beneficial to the interest of both society and the individual. But the desired synthesis gradually disintegrated during the nineteenth century and the truths of sincerity were lost to civilization as the ideal of authenticity became the dominant concern of the modern temper. The process finds its culmination in the recent doctrine, propounded by psychologists such as R. D. Laing and David Cooper, that madness is health, that insanity is a direct and appropriate response to the coercive inauthenticity of society.

Recognizing the difficulty of summarizing *Sincerity and Authenticity,* Irving Howe instead renders the service of putting Trilling's distinctions between sincerity and authenticity in intense focus:

> Sincerity involves aspiration, an effort to live a moral norm; authenticity directs us to a putative truth about ourselves that depends on our "essential" being, "beneath" and perhaps in disregard of moral norms—though it demands that we drive toward that "essential" being with an imperiousness that is very much akin to traditional moralism. Sincerity implies a living up to, authenticity a getting down into. Sincerity is a social virtue, a compact between me, myself, and you; authenticity is an assertion, a defiance, a claim

> to cut away the falsities of culture. It takes two to be sincere, only one to be authentic. Sincerity speaks for a conduct of *should;* authenticity for a potential of *is.* Sincerity is a virtue of public consciousness, authenticity a repudiation of its bad faith. Sincerity implies a recognition of our limits, authenticity asserts the self as absolute. We are to be persuaded toward sincerity, but stripped, shocked, and shamed into authenticity.[13]

This is a helpfully accurate and comprehensive tabulation extracted from Trilling's nuanced and involuted arguments. And the upshot of those arguments is that authenticity has replaced sincerity in our esteem and is the dark source of what he finds unsettling in modern literature.

Sincerity and Authenticity ends with a reaffirmation of the Freudian view expressed most significantly for Trilling in *Civilization and Its Discontents:* civilization is the field of a perennial struggle between the humane forces of rational control and the destructive forces of impulse. This struggle, originating within the individual psychic organization, manifests itself as well in the external social order. Trilling acknowledges that the Freudian theory of mind and society has at its core "a flagrant inauthenticity which it deplores but accepts as essential in the mental structure" (*SA,* 142). He then explains that "Freud, in insisting upon the essential immitigability of the human condition as determined by the nature of the mind, had the intention of sustaining the authenticity of human existence that formerly had been ratified by God. It was his purpose to keep all things from becoming 'weightless' " (*SA,* 144). It is an "authenticating imperative, irrational and beyond the reach of reason, that Freud wishes to preserve" (*SA,* 145). Freud was not religious, but his view is analogous to the tragic element in Judaism and Christianity. It seems clear that in affirming Freud's secular morality Trilling is expressing his own. The view he ascribes to Freud best supports his desired qualities of variousness, possibility, complexity, and difficulty. At the time of *The Liberal Imagination,* he saw literature as the human activity best expressing these qualities. In *Sincerity and Authenticity,* he sees literature as an accomplice in the promulgation of a misguided impulse to authenticity that encourages the divorce of self from society, the mental life from the outer world, and the autonomous self from necessity.

Sincerity and Authenticity is the product of a divided mind, a reactionary mind self-consciously attempting to appear impartial. This ambivalence is reflected in the style, which William M. Chace describes as "densely involuted. It is at once urbane, dark, and torpid. It reflects authorial hesitancies and anxieties. It issues from a mind that desires to pay homage to art and imagination but has grown to distrust the nature of imagination. It desires to praise intellect, but now sees intellect everywhere put to bad uses."[14] Geoffrey Hartman also finds problems in the "relaxed style" of the book and says that at times one yearns for more trenchant comments—like those of Irving Howe or Philip Rahv.[15] Norman Podhoretz, who spoke out forcefully against the radical culture of the sixties in *Breaking Ranks: A Political Memoir,* had great respect for Trilling but wished that his former teacher had been more direct and aggressive in denouncing the adversary culture. He accuses Trilling of being strategically careful in his late years. Trilling treated volatile topics, says Podhoretz, "yet so long did he spend in getting to the point, and so heavily did he load it with academic baggage, that its power to impress—and to offend—was almost entirely dissipated."[16] In writing about the radicalism of the sixties, Trilling, in Podhoretz's view, "increasingly seemed to use both the idea of complication and the prose embodying it not so much to clarify and deepen his own point of view as to disguise and hide it." *Sincerity and Authenticity* gives the impression of a writer "no longer trying 'to see the object as in itself it really is' but trying instead to conceal as much as reveal, to say something and to deny at the same time that he was really saying it, to take part in a battle while at the same time pretending to be above it."[17] Podhoretz suggests that such lack of clarity implies a lack of courage, but he is willing to accept Trilling's response that it was a matter of "fatigue" rather than cowardice. "Subjects and problems got presented in a way that made one's spirits fail," Trilling explained. "It wasn't that one was afraid to go into it, or afraid of opposition—I suppose I am speaking personally—but rather that in looking at the matter one's reaction was likely to be a despairing shrug."[18] Although Trilling is speaking here specifically of his response to the radicalism of the sixties, the fatigue he describes informed his reaction to modern culture in general during his late years.

Although *Sincerity and Authenticity* was, in general, courteously reviewed as the work of an elder statesman of criticism mining familiar ground, some adherents of what Trilling characterized as the adversary culture made some very pointed criticisms, charging him with evasion and withdrawal. Grant Webster, in his history of postwar American literary opinion, describes the book as Trilling's swan song, pointless and unilluminating, capping a career that was a retreat from contemporary life and a failure to cope with the new.[19] John Vernon, while acknowledging "the massive intelligence" and "brilliant insights" of the book, complains that "it exists on a level of abstraction that manages to ignore people's actual lives and the actual culture they live in." He faults it for not analyzing specific social ills and for failing to acknowledge madness as a viable response to an insane society. It gives us, he asserts, a one-sided picture "with the other side lopped-off by a kind of nostalgia for the past."[20] And the conservatism of *Sincerity and Authenticity* disappointed even some of Trilling's earlier admirers; but at the level of seriousness and breadth Trilling achieves in this book, terms like *liberal* and *conservative* cease to have much relevance.

On the other hand, those more sympathetic with Trilling's humanistic concerns consider *Sincerity and Authenticity* his crowning achievement. Tom Samet calls it Trilling's "most comprehensive, compelling, and eloquent inquiry into the complexities and vicissitudes of the life of the self," and insists that the "scrupulous neutrality" in presenting historical developments should not be mistaken for lack of engagement or refusal of the critical function.[21] Richard Sennett calls it "his greatest, and least appreciated book."[22] Irving Howe describes it as "deceptively modest in scale, though tremendously ambitious in reach." It is a wonderful book, he says, "precisely in its tentativeness, the way it perches at a given historical moment to dramatize through variations a deep, abiding theme."[23] One British reviewer speaks of "the joy of this splendid book." *Joy* seems a peculiar word, but he has in mind the pleasure the reader derives from the "richness and adroitness of the style" and the largeness with which Trilling treats "the deepest questions of man, life, and the world."[24] David L. Kubal makes a similar point in observing that the book, though depicting an alarming revision of the moral life, does not leave an abiding sense of pessimism. Its effect is "ironically liberating. For it provides us with an experience of mind in act, in the process of thought, which is in itself invigorating."[25]

Chapter Six
A Traditional Humanist in a Modernist World

To be adequate, any final assessment of Lionel Trilling must begin with the recognition that he was a cultural critic rather than a pure literary critic. The cultural critic works by standards different from those of the exclusively literary critic and should be judged accordingly. Exclusively literary critics perform a very narrow function, yet must have the broadest possible sympathies—must in theory be as eclectic as an auctioneer. They cannot let personal quirks or philosophical or political theories blur the precision of their responses. Cultural critics, on the other hand, can perform a far broader function with far narrower—or at least far more personal—views, their subject matter being in fact so large that if it is not harnessed to a point of view it becomes unwieldy. And though even for them literature can never be merely a tract, it can be an indicator, it can help determine the master currents of an age. Exclusively literary critics have, at least in one sense, greater latitude for mistakes. When they treat authors or works individually and on their own terms, their slipups are often less conspicuous, because they can be very wrong about Dickinson and yet very perceptive about Whitman. Cultural critics, on the other hand, put at risk the credibility of their shaping cultural vision each time they approach an individual subject as a cultural manifestation.

An adequate assessment of Trilling must also be aware of certain tensions inherent in his situation—the circumstances of his values and objectives in relation to his cultural environment. These tensions constitute a sort of complex which determined his characteristic methods, attitudes, and style and oriented his development. Perhaps the most significant of them was that he was essentially a conservative—a conserving mind—nurtured in a liberal-radical environment. A corollary to this was that he was a traditional humanist in an intellectual environment committed to modernism. Related to these tensions was his devotion to culture in conflict with his adversary stance toward the coercive power of culture. Moreover, he was a thoroughly literary mind haunted by a suspicion of literature. His repeated insistence that literature be a criticism of life is balanced in his writing by its counterpart: life is and ought to be a criticism of literature. He frankly confessed "to be a little skeptical of literature, impatient with it, or at least with the claims of literature to be an autonomous, self-justifying activity" (*LD,* 228). Finally, there was the opposition within his work that Jacques Barzun describes as "the desire to show the complexity that thought must attain in order to do reality justice and the need for lucid simplifying which teaching undergraduates or reviewing books for general readers entails."[1] It is no wonder Trilling felt that "in the intellectual life there ought to be frequent occasions for the exercise of ambivalence" (*GF,* 128).

As Trilling was fond of observing, critics worth reading will make systematic errors due to some persistently or obsessively skewed aspect of their perception, which is necessarily bound up with their power of seeing what truth they do see (*GF,* 114; *LD,* 83; *SLS,* 379). "We properly judge a critic's virtue not by his freedom from error but by the nature of the mistakes he does make, for he makes them, if he is worth reading, because he has in mind something beside his perceptions about art in itself—he has in mind the demands he makes upon life; and those critics are most to be trusted who allow these demands in all their particularity, to be detected by their readers" (*PMA,* 184). In an age of structuralism and poststructuralism, this notion of the critic seems antiquated if not obsolete, but it applies precisely to Trilling himself, who rigorously subordinated his perceptions of art to his demands upon life and made those demands explicit. Therefore, a judgment of his achievement requires an awareness of the nature of his mistakes.

One of his limitations has to do with his habitual use of *we.* Many readers do not want to be included within the reference of that pronoun. Graham Hough, for example, separates himself because of the "overpowering pedagogical tone" of Trilling's discourse and because he finds the style "monotonously apocalyptic." He argues that modern writers are not all as Trilling portrays them.[2] Trilling conceded truth in the criticism that the *we* in his writings shifts from the people of our time, to Americans in general, to a very narrow class consisting of New York intellectuals. He refers to it as "a minor rhetorical device, employed in the effort to describe the temper of our age." He notes the influence of New York intellectuals and insists that between this small class and analogous ones anywhere else in the world "there is pretty sure to be a natural understanding" (*BC,* viii–ix). Norman Podhoretz tries to defend Trilling's use of *we* by arguing that although Trilling spoke from his experience as a member of a small community, that community was concerned with a great issue affecting the educated American middle class in general: alienation.[3] But this misses the point of the criticism. A good part of the educated American middle class is not alienated, unless it is from the concerns and fashions of New York intellectuals. The truth is that Trilling's *we* often refers to the secular community of the contemporary liberal intelligentsia, and for many living in America's heartland that is a singularly provincial and unrepresentative community. His identification with fashionable views of a small group of New York intellectuals sometimes made him vulnerable to fretting over matters many educated Americans would consider insignificant or even absurd—R. D. Laing's notion of madness as health, for example.

Another of Trilling's limitations derived from his tendency to enter into everything without losing his balance. This impossible undertaking results in a pervasive inconclusiveness as regards ultimates. The questions he asked were profoundly important, but he provided disappointingly few positive and specific answers. His cultural diagnoses are often first-rate; but of such a penetrating diagnostician, we expect the ultimate transition from diagnostic to judicial statements, and in this we are often disappointed. He was greatly concerned about the sensibility, responsiveness, and general intelligence about literature of his liberal audience, but he seldom had any particular doctrine to offer—only an attitude of mind. We are always sure of his intelligence, but not always sure about what specific conclusions that intelligence has reached. He repeatedly observed that man is neither beast nor angel, but if this is true, where does man fit? Where should he turn? Nathan A. Scott, Jr., says these questions needed to be posed to Trilling forcefully because his characteristic strategems "simply subtilize his central problem into a matter disposable by a graceful pirouette of rhetoric." His work needed to be completed by a large constructive philosophical effort, suggests Scott, "and the gingerliness with which he has skirted this final aspect of his enterprise makes for the special sort of disappointment which his work calls forth."[4]

Others have echoed this charge of evasiveness. Graham Hough, in objecting to Trilling's tentativeness, observes that "to indulge so consistently in these hesitations, dissociations, and withdrawals is not, it seems to me, to stand beyond one's culture, but simply to occupy a very indeterminate position with it."[5] Mark Shechner praises Trilling's resistance to system, but suggests that he was sometimes evasive: "Applying rhetorical etiquette is not the same thing as defending complex and subtle ideas against reductionism, and what passes in Trilling for balance or negative capability or a full and judicious view of situations is sometimes just a pulling of punches."[6] W. J. Harvey suspects that the charm of Trilling's prose may mask a weakness in argument, and that "the immense, impressive but somehow unfunctional barrage of cultural references" may be a facade concealing the evasion of judgment: In place of judgment, "we are offered a kind of moral or cultural generalization which sees value or interest in practically everything."[7] It is possible, in short, to admire Trilling's dialectical method and wise awareness of complexity and yet feel uncomfortable that they are ultimately unanchored to a definite philosophical or religious commitment.

Related to the question of evasion is Trilling's habit of treating subjects at a high level of abstraction. Some complain that he turned modern literature into an abstraction. He was obsessed with the modern temper but unfortunately did not point it out specifically and concretely in particular works. In other words, in looking at his own time he manifested that tendency he so often deplored of ignoring the actual, material, and concrete commonplaces. Instead he treats an aura, a spirit, a vague intellectual temperament. And, in view of his preoccupation with contemporary culture and particularly with connecting literature with contemporary moral life, it is puzzling that he wrote almost no serious, detailed, specific criticism of major modern authors, even those he admired.

The most significant omission in Trilling's work is his failure, despite his historical predisposition, to recognize the vital significance of the continuing secularization of culture and the gradual withdrawal of God that have characterized the West since the seventeenth century. Although he often wrote of religion as an element in culture, his perspective was completely secular and incapable of deep or sympathetic response to the religious experience. This is not to say that he lacked the sort of yearning for absolutes that religion often satisfies. René Wellek correctly notes that "there is in Trilling in spite of his historicism and relativism a strong yearning for absolutes, if not religious or transcendental in any way, then for moral and aesthetic absolutes."[8] Graham Hough likens this yearning in Trilling to Emerson's transcendentalism: "a sort of fixed hopefulness for which no grounds whatever are given; the positing of an ideal which is flatly contradicted by all actual tendencies and circumstances."[9] Trilling's early description of Arnold has an uncanny aptness when applied to himself in his later years: "Self-cultivation in loneliness, in the face of the degeneracy of the world, with reference to some eternal but ill-defined idea—it is a familiar burden of Matthew Arnold's communion with himself" (*MA,* 118). Since Trilling confined himself to the tradition of modern secular thought, and since that tradition abrogated the basis for any eternal, fixed principles, he had no choice but to give priority to the virtue of flexibility and irresolution of mind. His procedure, Nathan A. Scott, Jr., perceptively remarks, "seems in a strange way to be like that of the great theological doctors of the Negative Way: it often appears primarily to involve the method of aposiopesis, of saying (against the Modern Anthology)—'Not that . . . and not that . . . and not that. . . .' "[10]

The more a moralist turns away from an eternal pattern and the possibility of transcendental sanctions, the more he has to rely for his moral standard upon some experienced and wise individual. This was the case with Trilling and accounts for the element of hero worship in his writing—a pressing need for exemplars that sometimes involved idiosyncratic interpretation of those models. Trilling's Keats and Freud, for example, may be scarcely recognizable to others acquainted with them. His unflagging devotion to Freud is particularly problematic. As William Barrett observes, Freud and psychoanalysis look much different to us now from what they did to Trilling in 1950. Sexual liberation has turned into sexual nihilism, and deeper questions have arisen: "And for such perplexities Freud does not offer a philosophy of life nor even an adequate theory of the human Self. His tripartite map of the soul—ego, id, and superego—is an arid and artificial construction."[11] Whether one agrees with this view of Freudian psychology, Trilling's faith in his version of Freudianism as a source of moral authority is problematic.

The obvious objections that recent critical theorists would make to Trilling's strictly instrumental theory of language and his circumvention of the questions raised by modern linguistics and hermeneutics are too complex to summarize here. It is sufficient to remark that his content-oriented approach leaves out of consideration many aspects of literature that are felt by others to be of the first importance.

How much Trilling's mistakes matter depends ultimately upon the interests, values, and prejudices of his readers; but there is one sense in which the errors are implicated in his achievement. If he had not slighted or ignored some aspects of the critical function, he could not have made the brilliant and valuable achievements he did in other aspects. If he had not rigorously adhered to the position in between, to the dialectical posture, to negative capability—even if this entailed evasion and irresolution—he could not have demonstrated so persuasively the dangers of absolutist and reductive systematizing in literature, politics, and culture. If he had not slighted close reading and aesthetic analysis, he could not have illuminated so brilliantly the interrelationship of literature and culture. If his temperament had not been so completely secular, he could not have brought into focus, as Nathan A. Scott, Jr., has pointed out, "the nub of that central perplexity which is felt by the people whose placement in history has permitted them to be deeply affected by the legacy of Rousseau and Marx and Freud." Because he did, says Scott, he "makes a kind of *exemplum* which, in some small degree perhaps, we fail to contemplate at our peril."[12]

Trilling's ultimate conviction was that the life of the mind is the life most worth living. He made this conviction contagious. As his publisher, William Jovanovich, states in his foreword to *Prefaces to The Experience of Literature,* "I found that reading Lionel Trilling one feels himself to be very intelligent." His example of the reasonable man persuading others to the advantages of reason, his courteous mediating between opposing viewpoints and traditions, his patient insistence on the flexible and comprehensive mind as a basis for a viable social order—all these are inspiriting. Steven Marcus saw a spiritual heroism in his "exigency and minimalism—his ability to affirm, without illusion, qualities and virtues that his own group, his own culture, his own audience had largely given up as being at once excessive in their demands upon us and insufficient in the gratification they return."[13] Trilling believed that criticism consists in the free play of mind over a subject. Immediate practical effects are not necessary or even desirable. "The spectacle of the human mind in action is vivifying," he said; "the explorer need discover nothing so long as he has adventured. Energy, scope, courage—these may be admirable in themselves. And in the end these are often what endure best."[14]

These are the elements of Trilling that endure best. As Lewis Leary says in tribute, "it is the spirit of Lionel Trilling which lives on—his sweetness, grace, compulsive high seriousness and compassion, his insistence that mind can matter, and that literature can feed mind and make possible the luxury of the discovery of self."[15] In Nietzsche's phrase, Trilling was "one of the spirits of yesterday—and the day after tomorrow." While he adapted as best he could to his age, he looked fondly back at the nineteenth century, and maintained an unexpressed, or at least only rarely expressed, hope that the future would bring a revival of the humanistic values he cherished.

Notes and References

Chapter One

1. Irving Howe, *A Margin of Hope* (San Diego: Harcourt Brace Jovanovich, 1982), 174.
2. Philip French, *Three Honest Men: Edmund Wilson, F. R. Leavis, and Lionel Trilling* (Manchester: Carcanet New Press, 1980), 101.
3. William Barrett, *The Truants: Adventures Among the Intellectuals* (Garden City, N.Y.: Anchor Press/Doubleday, 1982), 177.
4. In *Art, Politics, and Will: Essays in Honor of Lionel Trilling,* ed. Quentin Anderson, Stephen Donadio, and Steven Marcus (New York: Basic Books, 1977), 278.
5. Douglas Bush, quoted in William M. Chace, "Lionel Trilling: The Contrariness of Culture," *American Scholar* 48 (1978–79):49.
6. John Holloway, "Sincerely, Lionel Trilling," *Encounter* 41 (September 1973):67.
7. Irving Howe, *Celebrations and Attacks: Thirty Years of Literary and Cultural Commentary* (New York: Harcourt Brace Jovanovich, 1979), 219.
8. French, *Three Honest Men,* 75.
9. Chace, "Lionel Trilling," 50.
10. Clifford Geertz, "Found in Translation: On the Social History of the Moral Imagination," in *Local Knowledge: Further Essays in Interpretive Anthropology* (New York: Basic Books, 1983).
11. Steven Marcus, in *Art, Politics, and Will,* 277.
12. Norman Podhoretz, *Breaking Ranks* (New York: Harper & Row, 1979), 280.
13. "The Life of the Novel," *Kenyon Review* 8 (1946):658.
14. R. P. Blackmur, "The Politics of Human Power," *Kenyon Review* 12 (1950):663, 665, 667.
15. Edward Joseph Shoben, Jr., *Lionel Trilling* (New York: Frederick Ungar, 1981), 55.
16. Richard Sennett, "On Lionel Trilling," *New Yorker,* 5 November 1979, 209.
17. R. W. B. Lewis, "Lionel Trilling and the New Stoicism," *Hudson Review* 3 (1950):313.
18. Tom Samet, "Lionel Trilling and the Social Imagination," *Centennial Review* 23 (1979):169–70.
19. Chace, "Lionel Trilling," 56.

20. The primary source of biographical information is Diana Trilling's "Lionel Trilling: A Jew at Columbia," which first appeared in the March 1979 issue of *Commentary* and was later included as an appendix in *SLS*. Mark Krupnick, in "Lionel Trilling, 'Culture,' and Jewishness," *Denver Quarterly* 18 (1983):106–22, provides additional information about the family acquired through telephone conversations with Trilling's sister, Mrs. Harriet Schwartz. Mrs. Schwartz's account of her father's education and business success is more complimentary and perhaps less objective than Diana Trilling's.

21. Elinor Grumet, "The Menorah Idea and the Apprenticeship of Lionel Trilling" (Ph.D. diss., University of Iowa, 1979), 146–47.

22. Ibid., 116–17.

23. Diana Trilling is presently writing a combined autobiography and biography of her husband that will undoubtedly illuminate some of the puzzling questions about the development of his thought.

24. Alfred Kazin, *New York Jew* (New York: Alfred A Knopf, 1978), 43, 192.

25. Mark Shechner, "The Elusive Trilling (Part I)," *Nation,* 17 September 1977, 248.

26. Trilling to Allen Ginsberg, 11 September 1945; Trilling Papers, Butler Library, Columbia University.

27. Robert Langbaum, "The Importance of *The Liberal Imagination,*" *Salmagundi* 41 (Spring 1978):65.

28. Irving Howe, quoted in French, *Three Honest Men,* 77.

29. Philip Lopate, "Remembering Lionel Trilling," *American Review* 25 (October 1976):150.

30. Mark Shechner, "Psychoanalysis and Liberalism: The Case of Lionel Trilling," *Salmagundi* 41 (Spring 1978):29.

31. Kazin, *New York Jew,* 42.

32. Jacques Barzun, quoted in French, *Three Honest Men,* 101–2.

33. William Phillips, *A Partisan View: Five Decades of the Literary Life* (New York: Stein & Day, 1983), 75.

34. Barrett, *The Truants,* 162, 167.

35. Jacques Barzun, "Remembering Lionel Trilling," *Encounter* 47 (September 1976):82–83.

36. Letter to Simon Noveck, 18 November 1954; quoted in Grumet, "The Menorah Idea," 139.

37. Barzun, "Remembering," 83.

38. "A Personal Memoir," in *From Parnassus: Essays in Honor of Jacques Barzun,* ed. Dora B. Weiner and William R. Keylor (New York: Harper & Row, 1976), xvii.

39. Grumet, "The Menorah Idea," 95.

40. Ibid., 148.

41. Interview with Diana Trilling, 13 June 1985.

42. Grumet, "The Menorah Idea," 96.
43. Ibid., 107.
44. Ibid., 109, 111–12.
45. Ibid., 127–28.
46. "A Too Simple Simplicity," *Menorah Journal* 17 (December 1929):293.
47. "Despair Apotheosized," *Menorah Journal* 17 (October 1929):91–94.
48. "A Light to the Nations," *Menorah Journal* 14 (April 1928):402.
49. Grumet, "The Menorah Idea," 115.
50. Howe, *A Margin of Hope* 137.
51. Phillips, *A Partisan View,* 74.
52. Mark Shechner, "Psychoanalysis and Liberalism," 31.
53. Howe, *A Margin of Hope,* 139.
54. "The Mind of Robert Warshow," *Commentary,* June 1961, 502–3.
55. Grumet, "The Menorah Idea," 163.
56. Kazin, *New York Jew,* 46.
57. Trilling to Barzun, 26 March 1927; Barzun Papers, Butler Library, Columbia University.
58. W. M. Frohock, "Lionel Trilling and the American Reality," *Southwest Review* 45 (1960):224, 226–27.
59. A notebook entry for 5 May 1936 reveals that Trilling received this information at secondhand from Jacques Barzun, who reported to Trilling his conversation with Harrison Ross Steeves, chairman of the Columbia College English Department ("From the Notebooks of Lionel Trilling," *Partisan Review* 51–52 [1984–85]:498).
60. Trilling to Barzun, 26 July 1935; Barzun Papers.
61. According to Sidney Hook in a brief account in the January 1979 issue of *Mainstream* ("Anti-Semitism in the Academy; Some Pages of the Past"), he provided Trilling with the strategy of confronting the Department chairman with the charge that he was being dismissed because he was a Jew. Diana Trilling makes no mention of Hook in her account. The differences in the accounts are not important. Hook, unfortunately for his credibility in this instance, misremembered who was English Department chairman at the time and uses the name Ernest Hunter Wright instead of Harrison Ross Steeves.
62. Barzun, "Remembering," 84.
63. Howe, *A Margin of Hope,* 172.
64. Lopate, "Remembering." 151, 153.
65. Ibid., 152.
66. French, *Three Honest Men,* 83.
67. John Hollander, quoted in ibid., 82.
68. Ibid., 82.
69. Lopate, "Remembering," 156.

70. Trilling to Barzun, 24 June 1937; Barzun Papers.

71. James Burkhart Gilbert, *Writers and Partisans: A History of Literary Radicalism in America* (New York: John Wiley & Sons, 1968), 165–66.

72. Jacques Barzun, quoted in French, *Three Honest Men,* 86.

73. Trilling to Barzun, 15 June 1939; Barzun papers.

74. Ransom to Trilling, 26 March 1940, 21 July 1940, and 16 June 1942; Trilling Papers.

75. Trilling to Barzun, 18 June 1942; Barzun Papers.

76. Howe, *A Margin of Hope,* 139, 136.

77. Phillips, *A Partisan View,* 298, 279.

78. Interview with Diana Trilling, 13 June 1985.

79. Grant Webster, *The Republic of Letters: A History of Postwar American Literary Opinion* (Baltimore: Johns Hopkins University Press, 1979), 257, 252.

80. David Daiches, "The Mind of Lionel Trilling," *Commentary,* July 1957, 66.

81. Chace, "Lionel Trilling," 58.

82. Trilling to Herbert L. Jacobson, 12 January 1959; Trilling Papers.

Chapter Two

1. Trilling to Barzun, 28 July 1938; Barzun Papers.

2. Trilling to Barzun, 15 June 1937; Barzun Papers.

3. Edmund Wilson, "Uncle Matthew," *New Republic,* 22 March 1939, 199–200.

4. Edward Sackville-West, quoted in W. S. Knickerbocker, review of *Matthew Arnold, Sewanee Review* 47 (1939):442.

5. Barzun to Trilling, 21 July 1938; Trilling Papers.

6. R. C. Bald, review of *Matthew Arnold, Yale Review* 28 (1939):858.

7. Knickerbocker, review of *Matthew Arnold,* 443.

8. C. F. Harrold, review of *Matthew Arnold, Modern Philology* 37 (1939):220.

9. Barzun, "Remembering," 83–84.

10. John Henry Raleigh's "Editor's Page: Matthew Arnold and Lionel Trilling," *Arnoldian* 3, no. 1 (Winter 1976):2–3.

11. Morton Dauwen Zabel, "A Forster Revival [review of *E.M. Forster*]," *Nation,* 7 August 1943, 158–59.

12. Donald Daiches, review of *E. M. Forster, Accent* 4 (1943):62.

13. E. B. Greenwood, "The Literary Criticism of Lionel Trilling," *Twentieth Century* 163 (1958):45.

14. William M. Chace, *Lionel Trilling: Criticism and Politics* (Stanford: Stanford University Press, 1980), 72.

15. Kazin, *New York Jew,* 222.

16. Trilling to Herbert L. Jacobson, 4 December 1943; Trilling Papers.

17. John Bayley, "Only Disconnect," review of *Selected Letters of E. M. Forster,* vol. 2, ed. Mary Lago and P. N. Furbank, *New York Review of Books,* 15 August 1985, 19.

18. Barrett, *The Truants,* 129.

19. Diana Trilling to Stephen L. Tanner, 12 September 1986.

20. Trilling to Herbert L. Jacobson, 22 July 1970; Trilling Papers.

Chapter Three

1. William Freedman, "Lionel Trilling and the Novel of Ideas," in *The Forties: Fiction, Poetry, Drama,* ed. Warren French (Deland, Fl.: Everett/ Edwards, 1969), 239.

2. Barzun, "Remembering," 86–87.

3. Shoben, *Lionel Trilling,* 52–54.

4. Interview with Diana Trilling, 13 June 1985.

5. E. M. Forster, *Howards End* (New York: Vantage Books, 1921), 187.

6. Diana Trilling, "The Other Night at Columbia: A Report from the Academy," *Partisan Review* 26 (1959):218.

7. Diana L. George, "Thematic Structure in Lionel Trilling's 'Of This Time, Of That Place,' " *Studies in Short Fiction* 13 (1976):2–3.

8. Trilling to Ginsberg, 20 October 1950; Trilling Papers.

9. W. Paul Elledge, "The Profaning of Romanticism in Trilling's 'Of This Time, Of That Place,' " *Modern Fiction Studies* 29 (1983):226.

10. John V. Hagopian, "The Technique and Meaning of Lionel Trilling's 'The Other Margaret,' " *Etudes Anglaises* 16 (1963):229.

11. Sister Estelle Casalandra, "The Three Margarets," *Sewanee Review* 81 (1973):235–36.

12. James T. Farrell, *Literature and Morality* (New York: Vanguard Press, 1946), 13–14.

13. Howe, *A Margin of Hope,* 158–59.

14. Phillips, *A Partisan View,* 19.

15. Diana Trilling, review of *The Auden Generation,* by Samuel Hynes, *New York Times Book Review,* 22 May 1977, 40.

16. Diana Trilling, "The Other Night at Columbia," 220.

17. Podhoretz, quoted in French, *Three Honest Men,* 92.

18. Chace, *Lionel Trilling,* 137–38.

19. Shechner, "Psychoanalysis and Liberalism," 13.

20. Freedman, "Lionel Trilling," 242.

21. "Determinist and Mystic," *Kenyon Review* 2 (1940):97.

22. Chester E. Eisinger, "Trilling and the Crisis of Our Culture," *University of Kansas City Review* 25 (1958):35.

23. Irving Howe, "On *The Middle of the Journey,*" *New York Times Book Review,* 22 August 1976, 31.

24. William M. Chace, "*The Middle of the Journey:* Death and Politics," *Novel* 10 (1976–77):143.

25. Freedman, "Lionel Trilling," 240.

26. Shechner, "Psychoanalysis and Liberalism," 18.

27. John McCormick, *Catastrophe and Imagination* (London: Longmans, Green, 1971), 84.

28. René Wellek, "The Literary Criticism of Lionel Trilling," *New England Review* 2 (1979):28.

29. Howe, "On *The Middle of the Journey,*" 31.

30. Robert Warshow, *The Immediate Experience* (Garden City, N.Y.: Doubleday, 1962), 43–44.

31. Daniel Aaron, quoted in French, *Three Honest Men,* 89.

32. Robert Boyer, "*The Middle of the Journey* and Beyond: Observations on Modernity and Commitment," *Salmagundi* 1, no. 4 (1966–67):8–18.

33. Shechner, "Psychoanalysis and Liberalism," 7.

34. Freedman, "Lionel Trilling," 247.

35. "Marianne Gilbert Barnaby," "Lionel Trilling: Modulations of Arnoldian Criticism at the Present Time" (Ph.D. diss., University of Connecticut, 1975), 69.

36. Ransom to Trilling, 27 September 1948 [?]; Trilling Papers.

37. Morton Dauwen Zabel, *Craft and Character in Modern Fiction* (New York: Viking, 1957), 315.

38. David L. Kubal, "Trilling's *The Middle of the Journey:* An American Dialectic," *Bucknell Review* 14 (1966):62–63.

39. Barzun, quoted in French, *Three Honest Men,* 91.

Chapter Four

1. Barzun, "Remembering," 39.

2. Shechner, "Psychoanalysis and Liberalism," 16.

3. William E. Cain, "Trilling in Our Time," *Virginia Quarterly Review* 54 (1978):567.

4. Howe, *Celebrations and Attacks,* 213.

5. Howe, *A Margin of Hope,* 229.

6. Nathan A. Scott, Jr., "Lionel Trilling's Anxious Humanism—The Search for 'Authenticity,'" in *Three American Moralists: Mailer, Bellow, Trilling* (Notre Dame: University of Notre Dame Press, 1973).

7. Lewis, "Lionel Trilling," 316–17.

8. Irving Howe, "Lionel Trilling: A Word of Remembrance," *Salmagundi* 35 (Fall 1976):5.

9. Joseph Frank, "Lionel Trilling and the Conservative Imagination," *Sewanee Review* 64 (1956):296; reprinted with an appendix in *Salmagundi* 41 (Spring 1978):32–54.

10. Trilling to Richard Chase, 7 September 1949; Trilling Papers.

11. "The Necessary Morals of Art," *Menorah Journal* 18 (February 1930):183–84.

12. D. H. Hirsch, "Reality, Manners and Mr. Trilling," *Sewanee Review* 72 (1964):425–27.

13. Introduction to *The Partisan Reader: Ten Years of Partisan Review, 1934–1944,* ed. William Phillips and Philip Rahv (New York: Dial Press, 1946), xiv.

14. Scott, "Lionel Trilling's Anxious Humanism," 182–83.

15. Interview with Diana Trilling, 13 June 1985.

16. Podhoretz, *Breaking Ranks,* 279.

17. Shechner, "Psychoanalysis and Liberalism," 11.

18. Cain, "Trilling," 569.

19. Chace, *Lionel Trilling,* 98.

20. "A Rejoinder to Mr. Barrett," *Partisan Review* 16 (1949):656.

21. "The Life of the Novel," *Kenyon Review* 8(1946):666.

22. Trilling to Barzun, 19 September 1961; Barzun Papers.

23. Wellek, "The Literary Criticism of Lionel Trilling," 26–49.

24. Trilling to Herbert L. Jacobson, 19 July 1949; Trilling Papers.

25. Langbaum, "The Importance of *The Liberal Imagination,*" 55, 57.

26. Ransom to Trilling, 4 September 1942; Trilling Papers.

27. Ransom to Trilling, 10 May 1945; Trilling Papers.

28. Ransom to Trilling, 16 November 1945; Trilling Papers.

29. Louis Leary, "Lionel Trilling 1905–1975," *Sewanee Review* 84 (1976):302.

30. Stephen Donadio, quoted in French, *Three Honest Men,* 104.

31. Howe, *A Margin of Hope,* 149.

32. Ibid., 145.

33. Langbaum, "The Importance of *The Liberal Imagination,*" 60.

34. Delmore Schwartz, "The Duchess' Red Shoes," *Partisan Review* 20 (1953):63.

35. Trilling to Chase, 7 September 1949; Trilling Papers.

36. Barzun Papers.

37. Interview with Diana Trilling, 13 June 1985.

38. Derek Stanford, "A Note on Literary Liberalism," *Contemporary Review* 205 (1964):402, 405.

39. Chace, *Lionel Trilling,* 147.

40. See, for example, Steven Marcus, "Lionel Trilling, 1905–1975," in *Art, Politics, and Will,* 266. See also the quotation from Morris Dickstein in French, *Three Honest Men,* 93.

41. Frank, "Lionel Trilling," 298, 308.

42. Phillips, *A Partisan View,* 72.

43. Chace, *Lionel Trilling,* 67.

44. Howe, *Margin of Hope,* 231.

45. Irving Howe, quoted in French, *Three Honest Men,* 93.

46. Phillips, *A Partisan View,* 72.

47. Delmore Schwartz, quoted in Barrett, *The Truants,* 165.

48. William Van O'Connor, "Lionel Trilling's Critical Realism," *Sewanee Review* 58 (1950):482.

49. Chace, *Lionel Trilling,* 67.

50. See, for example, Frank, "Lionel Trilling," 298; Paul West, "Romantic Identity in the Open Society: Anguished Self-Scrutiny Among the Writers," *Queens Quarterly* 65 (1959):582; and Shoben, *Lionel Trilling,* 106, 246.

51. Paul Elmer More, *Shelburne Essays,* Seventh Series (Boston: Houghton Mifflin, 1910), pp. 218, 219, 220.

52. Trilling to Barzun, 15 June 1938; Barzun Papers.

53. Blackmur, "The Politics of Human Power," 667.

54. Barrett, *The Truants,* 175.

55. Marcus, "Lionel Trilling," 270.

56. Schechner, "Psychoanalysis and Literature," 21.

57. Trilling to Van Doren, 30 August 1950; Trilling Papers.

58. Barrett, *The Truants,* 176.

59. Steven Marcus, quoted in French, *Three Honest Men,* 87.

60. Shechner, "Psychoanalysis and Literature," 22.

61. Ibid., 20–21.

62. Louis Fraiberg, *Psychoanalysis and American Literary Criticism* (Detroit: Wayne State University Press, 1960), 215.

63. Shechner, "Psychoanalysis and Literature," 23–24.

64. Shoben, *Lionel Trilling,* 199.

65. Denis Donoghue, "Trilling, Mind, and Society," *Sewanee Review* 86 (1978):172–73, 174.

66. Ibid., 170.

67. Helen Vendler, "Lionel Trilling and the Immortality Ode," *Salmagundi* 41 (Spring 1978):67.

68. Trilling to Ginsberg, 20 October 1950, 14 September 1948, 5 November 1952; Trilling Papers.

69. Shechner, "Psychoanalysis and Literature," 28.

70. Scott, *Three American Moralists,* 184, 186.

71. Jeffrey Robinson, "Lionel Trilling: A Bibliographic Essay," *Resources for American Literary Study* 8 (1978):146.

72. Samet, "Lionel Trilling," 164.

73. Mark Krupnick, "Lionel Trilling, Freud, and the Fifties," *Humanities in Society* 3 (1980):272.

74. Shechner, "Psychoanalysis and Literature," 19.

Chapter Five

1. Schwartz, "The Duchess' Red Shoes," 65.
2. Phillips, *A Partisan View,* 72.
3. "A Personal Memoir," xxi.
4. Quoted by Morris Dickstein in French, *Three Honest Men,* 97.
5. Howe, *Celebrations and Attacks,* 213–14.
6. "Sincerity and Authenticity: A Symposium," *Salmagundi* 41 (Spring 1978):105.
7. Quoted in Chace, "Lionel Trilling," 52–53.
8. "Sincerity and Authenticity: A Symposium," 106.
9. Donoghue, "Trilling," 182.
10. "Sincerity and Authenticity: A Symposium," 107–8.
11. Irving Babbitt, "Genius and Taste," in *Five Approaches of Literary Criticism,* ed. Wilbur Scott (New York: Collier-Macmillan, 1962), 39.
12. Barnaby, "Lionel Trilling," 144.
13. Howe, *Celebrations and Attacks,* 217–18.
14. Chace, "Lionel Trilling," 55.
15. Geoffrey Hartman, review of *Sincerity and Authenticity, New York Times Book Review,* 4 February 1973, 28.
16. Podhoretz, *Breaking Ranks,* 301.
17. Ibid., 298.
18. Quoted in ibid., 276.
19. Webster, *The Republic of Letters,* 257–59.
20. John Vernon, "On Lionel Trilling," *Boundary 2* 2 (1974):626, 630.
21. Tom Samet, "The Problematic Self: Lionel Trilling and the Anxieties of the Modern" (Ph.D., diss. Brown University, 1980), 155, 166.
22. Richard Sennett, "On Lionel Trilling," *New Yorker,* 5 November 1979, 207.
23. Howe, *Celebrations and Attacks,* 214.
24. John Holloway, "Sincerely, Lionel Trilling," *Encounter* 41 (September 1973):66.
25. David L. Kubal, "Lionel Trilling: The Mind and Its Discontents," *Hudson Review* 31 (1978–79):292–93.

Chapter Six

1. Barzun, "Remembering" 87.
2. Graham Hough, " 'We' and Lionel Trilling," *Listener* 75 (1955):760.
3. Podhoretz, *Breaking Ranks,* 281.
4. Scott, *Three American Moralists,* 211.
5. Hough, " 'We' and Lionel Trilling," 761.
6. Shechner, "Psychoanalysis and Liberalism," 24–25.

7. W. J. Harvey, "Editorial Notes: *Kulchur* and Culture in America," *Essays in Criticism* 10 (1960):447–48.

8. Wellek, "The Literary Criticism of Lionel Trilling," 48.

9. Hough, " 'We' and Lionel Trilling," 761.

10. Scott, *Three American Moralists,* 211.

11. Barrett, *The Truants: Adventures,* 176–77.

12. Scott, *Three American Moralists,* 154.

13. Marcus, "Lionel Trilling," 274.

14. "Eugene O'Neill," *New Republic,* 23 September 1936, 176.

15. Lewis Leary, "Lionel Trilling, 1905–1975," *Sewanee Review* 84 (1976):304.

Selected Bibliography

PRIMARY SOURCES

1. Critical Studies

E. M. Forster. Uniform Edition. New York: Harcourt Brace Jovanovich, 1980.

Matthew Arnold. Uniform Edition. New York: Harcourt Brace Jovanovich, 1977.

2. Fiction

The Middle of the Journey. Uniform Edition. New York: Harcourt Brace Jovanovich, 1980.

Of This Time, of That Place and Other Stories. Uniform Edition. New York: Harcourt Brace Jovanovich, 1980.

3. Collections of Essays and Lectures

Beyond Culture: Essays on Literature and Learning. Uniform Edition. New York: Harcourt Brace Jovanovich, 1978.

A Gathering of Fugitives. Uniform Edition. New York: Harcourt Brace Jovanovich, 1978.

The Last Decade: Essays and Reviews, 1965–75. Edited by Diana Trilling. Uniform Edition. New York: Harcourt Brace Jovanovich, 1977.

The Liberal Imagination: Essays on Literature and Society. Uniform Edition. New York: Harcourt Brace Jovanovich, 1979.

The Opposing Self: Nine Essays in Criticism. Uniform Edition. New York: Harcourt Brace Jovanovich, 1978.

Prefaces to The Experience of Literature. Uniform Edition. New York: Harcourt Brace Jovanovich, 1979.

Sincerity and Authenticity. Uniform Edition. New York: Harcourt Brace Jovanovich, 1980.

Speaking of Literature and Society. Edited by Diana Trilling. Uniform Edition. New York: Harcourt Brace Jovanovich, 1980.

4. Anthologies

The Experience of Literature. New York: Holt, Rinehart & Winston, 1967.

Literary Criticism: An Introductory Reader. New York: Holt, Rinehart & Winston, 1970.

The Portable Matthew Arnold. New York: Viking, 1949.

5. Uncollected Material

The Uniform Edition of The Works of Lionel Trilling contains 118 reviews, essays, and lectures. Approximately 140 items, mostly reviews, remain uncollected and are listed in the Barnaby bibliography cited below.

SECONDARY SOURCES

1. Bibliographies

Barnaby, Marianne Gilbert. "Lionel Trilling: A Bibliography, 1926–1972." *Bulletin of Bibliography* 31, no. 1 (January–March 1974):37–44.

Robinson, Jeffrey. "Lionel Trilling: A Bibliographic Essay." *Resources for American Literary Study* 8 (1978):131–56.

2. Books and Parts of Books

The following memoirs by New York intellectuals contain abundant mention of Trilling: William Barrett, *The Truants: Adventures Among the Intellectuals* (Garden City, N.Y.: Anchor Press/Doubleday, 1982); Irving Howe, *A Margin of Hope: An Intellectual Autobiography* (San Diego: Harcourt Brace Jovanovich, 1982); Alfred Kazin, *New York Jew* (New York: Alfred A. Knopf, 1978); William Phillips, *A Partisan View: Five Decades of the Literary Life* (New York: Stein & Day, 1983); Norman Podhoretz, *Making It* (New York: Random House, 1967) and *Breaking Ranks: A Political Memoir* (New York: Harper & Row, 1979).

Boyers, Robert. *Lionel Trilling: Negative Capability and the Wisdom of Avoidance.* Columbia: University of Missouri Press, 1977. A monograph focusing on two of Trilling's stories and his essay on James's *The Princess Casamassima.*

Chace, William M. *Lionel Trilling: Criticism and Politics.* Stanford: Stanford University Press, 1980. A perceptive study of Trilling's writing, not his life, with an emphasis on political-cultural ideas.

Fraiberg, Louis. *Psychoanalysis and American Literary Criticism.* Detroit: Wayne State University Press, 1960. Substantial chapter on Trilling's "creative extension of Freudian concepts."

French, Philip. *Three Honest Men: A Critical Mosaic, Edmund Wilson, F. R. Leavis, Lionel Trilling.* Manchester: Carcanet New Press, 1980. Revised transcript of a BBC radio program. Acquaintances of Trilling comment on his work and personality.

Krupnick, Mark. *Lionel Trilling and the Fate of Cultural Criticism.* Evanston: Northwestern University Press, 1986. A critical study of Trilling's intellectual development emphasizing the value of his cultural criticism as a salutary counterexample in the context of modern criticism.

Marcus, Steven. "Lionel Trilling, 1905–1975." In *Art, Politics, and Will: Essays in Honor of Lionel Trilling,* edited by Quentin Anderson, Stephen Donadio, and Steven Marcus. New York: Basic Books, 1977. An appraisal of Trilling's work from 1950 to his death, emphasizing his growing distrust of modern literature.

Scott, Nathan A., Jr. *Three American Moralists: Mailer, Bellow, Trilling.* Notre Dame: University of Notre Dame Press, 1973. An excellent survey of Trilling's writing focusing on his humanism. A religious perspective that is tolerant of but not sympathetic to Trilling's secularism.

Shoben, Edward Joseph, Jr. *Lionel Trilling: Mind and Character.* New York: Frederick Ungar, 1981. A clinical psychologist's sympathetic and illuminating consideration of Trilling's writings as a reflection of his character.

Raleigh, John Henry. *Matthew Arnold and American Culture.* Berkeley: University of California Press, 1961. A chapter surveying Trilling's writing in light of Arnold's influence upon him.

2. Articles

Adamowski, T. H. "Lionel Trilling: Modern Literature and Its Discontents." *Dalhousie Review* 55 (1975):83–92. Trilling's treatment of modern literature errs by being too abstract.

Barzun, Jacques. "Remembering Lionel Trilling." *Encounter* 47 (September 1976):82–88. Informative reflections on Trilling by one of his closest associates.

Blackmur, R. P. "The Politics of Human Power." *Kenyon Review* 12 (1950):663–73. Review of *The Liberal Imagination* that portrays Trilling as "an administrator of the affairs of the mind" with a conscious public voice.

Chace, William. "Lionel Trilling: The Contrariness of Culture." *American Scholar* 48 (1978–79):49–59. Well-informed overview intended to delineate the nature of Trilling's achievement.

Daiches, David. "The Mind of Lionel Trilling." *Commentary,* July 1957, 66–69. Trilling is the representative New York intellectual, which means he is very bright but a little out of touch with the actual situation in America at large.

Donoghue, Denis. "Trilling, Mind, and Society." *Sewanee Review* 86 (1978):161–86. Penetrating and subtle exposition of Trilling's interdependent concepts of mind and society.

Frank, Joseph. "Lionel Trilling and the Conservative Imagination." *Sewanee Review* 64 (1956):296–309. Reprinted with an appendix, *Salmagundi* 41 (1978):33–54. Charges Trilling with passivity and social quietism.

Frohock, W. M. "Lionel Trilling and the American Reality." *Southwest Review* 45 (1960):224–32. Charges that Trilling's understanding of America was incomplete because of a narrow New York perspective.

Hirsch, David H. "Reality, Manners, and Mr. Trilling." *Sewanee Review* 72 (1964):420–32. A criticism of Trilling's tendency to restrict the novel to the novel of manners, thus limiting the scope of "reality" with which it can deal.

Kim, Chrysostom. "Lionel Trilling on 'the Self in Its Standing Quarrel with Culture.' " *American Benedictine Review* 27 (1976):332–56. Three main themes: Trilling's ambivalence toward modern literature, his recognition of the cost of culture, and what he understands to be the mind of society.

Krupnick, Mark. "Lionel Trilling, 'Culture,' and Jewishness." *Denver Quarterly* 18, no. 3 (1983):106–22. An examination of Trilling's Jewish background and the way he distanced himself from Jewishness in his adult years.

———. "Lionel Trilling, Freud, and the Fifties." *Humanities in Society* 3 (1980):265–81. Beginning with *The Opposing Self,* under the influence of Freud Trilling develops a dull and passive concept of self.

Kubal, David. "Lionel Trilling" The Mind and Its Discontents." *Hudson Review* 31 (1978–79):279–95. Examines Trilling's mounting uneasiness with modernism during his later career.

Langbaum, Robert. "The Importance of *The Liberal Imagination.*" *Salmagundi* 41 (Spring 1978):55–65. Trilling's work complemented that of the New Critics, providing a needed examination of literature and social ideas.

Leary, Lewis. "Lionel Trilling 1905–1975." *Sewanee Review* 84 (1976):302–4. Brief summary of Trilling's distinctive achievement.

Lewis, R. W. B. "Lionel Trilling and the New Stoicism." *Hudson Review* 3 (1950–51):313–17. Review of *The Liberal Imagination* that describes Trilling's centrist position as "a new Stoicism."

Lopate, Phillip. "Remembering Lionel Trilling." *American Review* 25 (1976):148–78. One of Trilling's former students describes his impressions of Trilling as teacher.

O'Connor, William Van. "Lionel Trilling's Critical Realism." *Sewanee Review* 58 (1950):482–94. Review of *The Liberal Imagination* used as an occasion for describing the nature of Trilling's work to that point. Considers Trilling "the conscience of the intelligentsia of the left."

Robinson, Jeffrey. "Lionel Trilling and the Romantic Tradition." *Massachusetts Review* 20 (1979):211–36. An examination of Trilling's reading of the romantics and of his style in relation to them.

Samet, Tom. "Lionel Trilling and the Social Imagination." *Centennial Review* 23 (1979):159–84. An explanation of Trilling's pervasive social concerns based on thorough knowledge of Trilling's work.

———. "The Modulated Vision: Lionel Trilling's 'Larger Naturalism.' " *Critical Inquiry* 4 (1977–78):539–57. Drawing upon Arnold, Freud, and Forster, Trilling aims at a "larger naturalism" that synthesizes the legacies of the Enlightenment and the romantic movement.

———. "Trilling, Arnold and the Anxieties of the Modern." *Southern Quarterly* 16 (1977–78):191–209. An examination of how the influence of Arnold conditioned Trilling's struggle to cope with modernism.

Schwartz, Delmore. "The Duchess' Red Shoes." *Partisan Review* 20 (1953):55–73. Attacks Trilling's preoccupation with manners as being a concern with superficial social manners.

Sennet, Richard. "On Lionel Trilling." *New Yorker,* 5 November 1979, 204, 207–10, 215–17. Retrospective appreciative view that sees *Sincerity and Authenticity* as Trilling's greatest but least appreciated work.

Shechner, Mark. "Psychoanalysis and Liberalism: The Case of Lionel Trilling." *Salmagundi* 41 (Spring 1978):3–32. Broad and informative, giving special emphasis to Freud and liberalism but treating all the important aspects of Trilling's work.

Tanner, Tony. "Lionel Trilling's Uncertainties." *Encounter* 27 (1966):72–77. Trilling asks profoundly important questions about self and culture but provides no possible answers.

Wellek, Rene. "The Literary Criticism of Lionel Trilling." *New England Review* 2 (1979):26–49. An overview of Trilling's work.

4. Dissertations

Barnaby, Marianne Gilbert. "Lionel Trilling: Modulations of Arnoldian Criticism at the Present Time." Ph.D. dissertation, University of Connecticut, 1975. Explains how Trilling's Arnoldian faith in the civilizing effects of literature was tested and modified in his confrontation with modern literature.

Grumet, Elinor Joan. "The Menorah Idea and the Apprenticeship of Lionel Trilling." Ph.D. dissertation, University of Iowa, 1979. An examination of Trilling's involvement at the beginning of his career with the *Menorah Journal* and the movement to cultivate Jewish consciousness.

Index